The Jesus Clone

Christianity Explained

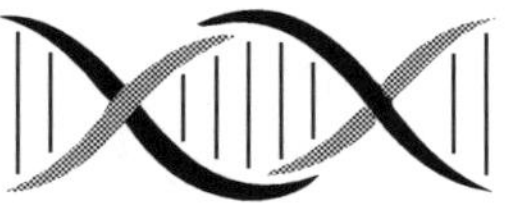

Emory Williams Jr.

WESTBOW PRESS®
A DIVISION OF THOMAS NELSON & ZONDERVAN

WestBow Press books may be ordered through booksellers or by contacting:

WestBow Press
A Division of Thomas Nelson & Zondervan
1663 Liberty Drive
Bloomington, IN 47403
www.westbowpress.com
844-714-3454

ISBN: 978-1-6642-3385-0 (sc)
ISBN: 978-1-6642-3386-7 (hc)
ISBN: 978-1-6642-3384-3 (e)

Library of Congress Control Number: 2021909260

Print information available on the last page.

WestBow Press rev. date: 05/21/2021

This book is dedicated to God, my Father, and Jesus Christ, my older brother.

To my parents, Emory Sr. and Nathailia, without whom this book would not have been possible. They not only provided a God-fearing, learning environment as I grew into adulthood, they have supported me throughout my life and have always been a source of great inspiration.

And to my wife, Claudia, who has been with me for forty-six years and counting.

Many people including friends, professors, pastors and even enemies have contributed to my life-long study of human nature and everything related to God.

I would not be the person I am today, or have the spiritual understanding I have, without their involvement in my life, and the guidance of the Holy Spirit.

Ultimately it is God who is responsible for my life and education, and for that I am eternally grateful. Without Him none of us would exist.

CONTENTS

PREFACE

It seems the media loves to report bad news. They focus on the negative issues of natural disasters, climate catastrophes, destructive riots, rising crime, corrupt politicians, pandemics, etc. Very little else appears to be newsworthy.

Many people feel the very fabric of society is unravelling around them. They see societies and cultures collapsing around the world. National and international conflicts are on the rise. Threats of war are on the horizon. People are afraid of what is happening.

If you worry about these things, and wonder what the future holds, this book is for you.

My goal is to help you better understand why these things happen; why there is so much evil in the world. More importantly, I want to help you better understand who Jesus Christ is, and what He has in store for you.

If you believe in God, this information may strengthen your faith and bring you peace of mind in these troubled times.

John 8:31–32 says,

> If you hold to my teaching, you are really my disciples. Then you will know the truth, and the truth will set you free. (NIV)

First Peter 3:15 says,

> Always be prepared to give an answer to everyone who asks you to give the reason for the hope that you have. (NIV)

This book is *my* answer!

– Emory Williams Jr.

INTRODUCTION

THE TITLE, *THE JESUS CLONE*, MAY SOUND SACRILEGIOUS, BUT I assure you it is not. With all due respect, reverence, and worship toward God and Jesus, I will explain the clone concept to give you a better understanding of them both. After we look at the clone concept, I'll present some personal speculation on how we were created and why our lives are what they are. Then we'll examine exactly what the Bible says, and what Christianity is all about. Appropriate scriptures and factual references are interspersed throughout to support my position.

There is no hidden agenda here, no ulterior motive. It is not my goal to convert you to a particular church or religious doctrine. I simply hope to give you things to consider as you follow your journey of faith.

As you begin reading you will notice I've written in a first-person style, speaking directly to you, the reader. This may not be the preferred style of writing, but it was important to me that you and I have this conversation. I would like you to hear what I have to say, then meditate on it and either agree or disagree. If you disagree with my take on what is meant by the Bible scriptures, then please stop and prove me wrong. I want you to be skeptical! You don't need to prove it to me, just prove it to yourself.

The Bible is consistent throughout with no contradictions, even though some people believe there are contradictions. When taken in context with all other related scriptures, apparent contradictions simply disappear. In other words, if one scripture appears to say one thing, and twenty-five other scriptures say the opposite thing, then the one scripture must be reconsidered to rectify the apparent contradiction. It is the one scripture that has been misunderstood, not the twenty-five.

This is a book of faith for two reasons. I have faith that this information is correct, according to my understanding, and what I believe to be inspiration by the Holy Spirit. If in the future it is determined to contain errors or misunderstandings, that is okay because some of this material is opinion, some is speculation. I do not presume to speak on behalf of God, I speak of my own accord based upon my understanding of the information He has provided us.

Human understandings change but God, His faithfulness, and His word never change. The quotes from the Bible will not change but our understanding of them may change. I know my salvation is secure whether I am right in these speculations or not.

This is also a book to help increase your faith as the reader. It is not an attempt to convert anyone to Christianity. It is written for people who already believe in God, or sincerely want to.

I will make no attempt to prove the existence of God, or that the Bible is His inspired word.[1] I assume this to be true, otherwise this book would be impossibly long and tedious. There are untold numbers of books written to prove or disprove the existence of God and the authenticity of the Bible. As it says, "Of making many books there is no end, and much study wearies the body."[2]

Some people believe in evolution. Many evolutionists attempt to prove God does not now, nor ever did, exist. The evolutionary concept is basically an attempt to prove that everything in existence, now or in the past, simply "popped" into existence without the need for a Creator.

Some believe in evolution and absolutely do not believe in God. If that is your belief, then this book is probably not for you. You have your science, your references, and your deep-rooted beliefs. The

---

[1] 2 Timothy 3:16.

[2] Ecclesiastes 12:12.

information contained herein will probably not help you. You may need to go elsewhere.

Others believe in God and a literal translation of the Bible. In other words, they believe God created everything in a literal six days, as recorded in Genesis. There are many resources, such as the Institute for Creation Research,[3] that support this position, work to prove science is wrong, and prove the Bible is absolute fact. If this is your belief, then you may find this book interesting.

Still others believe in God, but they also believe in the archeological/geological/scientific/astronomical evidence for billions of years of evolution as provided by science, and they can't quite figure out how to fit the concepts together. If this is your position, then the information in this book may help you answer a lot of questions to your own personal satisfaction, just as it has for me.

It is not my purpose to prove or disprove either of these opinions rather, in this book I will present a middle-of-the-road perspective that is intended to get you thinking.

Beginning in chapter two we address those of you who are struggling with a belief in God but are also confused as to how God fits with evolutionary evidence you feel you cannot dismiss.

Ultimately, it comes down to a personal decision to believe in God and accept His word based upon faith. By beginning with the assumption that you, the reader, already believe in both God and the Bible, we can get straight to the heart of the matter without wasting endless, unnecessary arguments.

Regardless of which of the above schools of thought you fit in; the bottom line is that our salvation does not depend upon one of these beliefs over the other. Our salvation comes from Jesus Christ alone. It is not determined by how we think everything came into existence, but by our faith in Him.

We were created in the image of God,[4] with the intent that we

---

[3] Icr.org.

[4] Genesis 1:26–27.

would eventually understand God and enter eternal life with Him as His children.[5] This book is an attempt to further that understanding in us all.

Over the course of my life, with many tedious years of study and prayer, I have been able to clarify my own thoughts and come to a more complete understanding of God and the Bible.

I hope you will take what I have written for what it is: Simply an attempt to help you better understand God and to be at peace with that understanding. These are my thoughts and understandings. This is how I have been able to achieve personal peace with my Creator, with my life, and with fellow human beings. I believe these ideas have been shaped by the Holy Spirit.

It is also my hope that if you do not already have a relationship with your Creator God, this will help you come to know Him. If you already have a relationship with God, then this book may help to increase your faith.

This is not intended for religious scholars. I do not present this as an authoritative work with endless proofs. There is no proof for some of these subjects until God chooses to reveal Himself in person to everyone, but I will present many appropriate references, primarily directly from the Bible, to support my position.

If you understand and agree with this material, then you will likely experience higher levels of faith and peace in your life. If you don't agree with it, then I wish you well. There are no hard feelings. No "I'm right and you're wrong" sentiment. You may have come to grips with your life and your Creator in a different manner. We will all fully understand when God determines the time is right.

This book contains scriptural fact (KJV, NKJV and NIV translations cited throughout) as well as speculation. When scripture is quoted it is fact. The speculation is mine. Please do not confuse the two.

The footnotes are references to scriptures that support my arguments. I encourage you to take time to stop and read each of the

---

[5] Ephesians 1:4–5.

scriptures contained in the footnotes, as you encounter them in the body of the text, rather than waiting till you finish as this will make the most sense. As you read the scriptures in context you will find I have not twisted any of the meanings simply to fit my arguments.

The appendix contains all the scriptures listed under footnotes (in chronological order according to the Bible) so you do not need a Bible handy when you're reading. However, it is always a good idea to verify the scriptures in your own Bible translation in case I have made any errors. And remember, I use several different Bible versions due to their clarity. If what I have placed in the appendix does not exactly match your Bible translation check one of the other translations listed here in the introduction.

Do not take my word for it, or anyone else's word for it. And please, do not believe any priest or pastor just because he is a priest or pastor. "Prove all things and hold fast to that which is good!"[6] Pray for the Holy Spirit to guide your understanding.

As you read this book remember, our salvation only depends upon one thing; whether by faith we accept Jesus Christ as our personal Savior and express that belief through godly love or not.[7] We cannot earn salvation. The Holy Spirit (as well as Faith, God's grace, peace, eternal life, and many other things) is a gift from God.[8]

Beliefs vary from denomination to denomination which means they cannot all be correct when many of their beliefs are contradictory. Unfortunately, many preachers today (especially radio and television preachers) try to get your attention by preaching about God's wrath. They threaten you with the fear of eternal damnation and torment in the fires of hell. The result is often a disingenuous conversion. When faced with the prospect of hell, people can be easily manipulated. Churches tend not to focus on God's love, they tend to focus on His wrath.

---

[6] 1 Thessalonians 5:21.

[7] Galatians 5:6.

[8] Acts 2:38; Acts 10:45; Romans 6:23; Ephesians 2:8; Ephesians 4:7; James 1:17–18; John 14:26–27.

Jesus did not preach hell fire and brimstone to get people to follow him. In the Sermon on the Mount, He said the poor in spirit, those who mourn, the meek, those who hunger and thirst for righteousness, the merciful, the pure in heart, the peacemakers, et al., were all blessed.[9] He did not threaten them with hell.

Isn't it interesting that when he finished, the crowds said He taught as one who had authority and not as their teachers of the law?[10]

It seems that today's preachers don't focus on the *good* news of the gospel. Instead, they may as well be saying, "Listen to me and do what I say, or you will burn in hell forever."

That doesn't sound like the good news that Jesus spoke of.

My hope is to help you better understand the good news that Jesus brought and show you how much God loves you.

This book represents a journey I have been on for many years. I hope you will now join me on this journey, all the way to the end.

---

[9] Matthew 5:3–12.

[10] Matthew 7:28–29.

PART I

THE CLONE

CHAPTER 1

THE CLONE

PLEASE DO NOT BE OFFENDED BY THE WORD *CLONE* IN REFERENCE to Jesus Christ. The Oxford dictionary defines a clone as, "an organism or cell, or group of organisms or cells, produced asexually from one ancestor or stock, to which they are genetically identical." The word clone is not derogatory; it is simply a scientific description.

Jesus is the *first*, and *only*, perfect clone of God. But before you stop reading because you believe I am blaspheming God the Father, the Son, and the Holy Spirit, let me explain.

Our God is One as taught by the Bible. That sounds simple. There is only one God (God the Father), not two or three. What does "One" mean? We could discuss that question alone all day. When God created man, He said a man should leave his father and mother and cleave unto his wife and the two shall be *one*.[11] The Hebrew word for *one* used here is the same word describing God as One in other parts of scripture.

So, were Adam and Eve one person or two? Obviously, they were two, but it was meant that they should become *one*. What does that mean? Were they to somehow morph into a unique new creature

[11] Genesis 2:24; Matthew 19:4–5.

through sexual relations over time? Were they to think alike? Were they to live as one person? Was one of them supposed to forfeit their personality and be assimilated by the other? Were the children they produced to be considered the *one* product of the two? These are all debatable issues.

Look around at your married friends. Would you consider them as *one*? Do they seem happy? Probably some do and some don't. What traits would you identify in those who are happy? Do they share common interests? Do they spend time together? Do they enjoy each other's company?

Probably, all these things and more.

How about those who are not happy? Do they respect each other? Are they faithful to each other? Do they truly love each other? Most likely the answer is no.

So, the absence of *one-ness* in marriage is easy to identify isn't it? If two people truly love each other they are concerned about each other's well-being. They share goals, dreams, and beliefs.

That is the type of marriage God has in mind for us.

Jesus said, "I and My Father are One"[12] but He also prayed that the disciples should become one, when He said, "as You, Father are in Me, and I in You; that they also may be one in Us."[13] Exactly what does this mean? My opinion is not necessarily better than that of anyone else who has an opinion, but I believe it means unity of spirit, unity of beliefs, unity of loving each other, complete and unreserved dedication, and commitment to obey the law of love and to worship God.

To examine this issue further we need to ask another question. Just who is Jesus Christ?

According to the book of John, "In the beginning was the Word, and the Word was with God, and the Word was God."[14] It also says,

[12] John 10:30.

[13] John 17:21.

[14] John 1:1.

"The Word became flesh and made His dwelling among us."[15] This was an incredible miracle.

Consider this. You have probably read about or seen movies about, the legendary detective Sherlock Holmes. He was a character invented by and written about by Sir Arthur Conan Doyle. When movies began to be made, an actor by the name of Basil Rathbone was one of the actors chosen to play the part of Sherlock. If you are old enough to remember the early movies you will probably visualize Mr. Rathbone when you think of Sherlock Holmes.

As an actor, Basil Rathbone personified all the words that Mr. Doyle wrote. He did his best to bring that character to life.

Jesus was not acting. Jesus *is* the actual, full, and complete personification of the Word of God.[16]

God's Word did not just assume human form as an actor portraying a part or as an alien from science fiction movies. The Word of God actually *became* flesh! Jesus was both God (the original Greek word used here for "God" (*theos*) can be translated as *divine* or *divinity*, for those of you who wish to research the subject) and man, and He voluntarily submitted Himself to crucifixion so we would have an example of God's love toward us and begin to understand the true meaning of love. I believe *this* is the mystery spoken of by Paul the apostle.[17]

When the Word became Jesus Christ, I believe He was born as a new and distinct person.[18] If not, how can the New Testament continually refer to Jesus (the Son and the Lamb) and God (the Father) as two distinct entities?[19]

Many scriptures seem to make this especially clear, and I think a few are worth quoting here.

---

[15] John 1:14.

[16] John 1:14.

[17] 1 Corinthians 2:6–8; Ephesians 1:4–12.

[18] John 5:26–27.

[19] Matthew 26:53; Mark 13:32; John 5:17; John 14:23; John 16:23; John 20:17; Romans 8:15–17; 1 Corinthians 15:22–28; 1 Peter 3:21–22; Revelation 3:21; 20:6; 21:22; etc.

Matthew 26:39 says Jesus "fell with His face to the ground and prayed, 'My Father, if it is possible, may this cup be taken from me. Yet not as I will but as you will.'" If Jesus and God the Father are the same person, then this scripture doesn't make sense. There must be a distinction between the two.

John 8:16–18 (emphasis added) says,

> I stand with the Father, who sent me. In your own Law it is written that the testimony of two witnesses is true. *I am one who testifies for myself; my other witness is the Father, who sent me.*

First John 2:1 (emphasis added) says, "But if anybody does sin, *we have one who speaks to the Father in our defense – Jesus Christ, the righteous One.*" Does that mean Jesus will be talking to Himself about us or will He talk to the Father?

First Corinthians 15:22–28 (emphasis added) says,

> For as in Adam all die, so in Christ all will be made alive. But each in his own turn: Christ, the firstfruits; then, when He comes, those who belong to Him. Then the end will come, when He hands over the kingdom to God the Father after He has destroyed all dominion, authority and power. For He must reign until He has put all His enemies under His feet. The last enemy to be destroyed is death. For He has put everything under His feet. Now when it says that everything has been put under Him, *it is clear that this does not include God Himself, who put everything under Christ. When He has done this, then the Son Himself will be made subject to Him who put everything under Him,* so that God may be all in all.

Without an understanding that God the Father and Jesus Christ the Son are two distinct persons this scripture does not make sense does it?

Revelation 3:21 (emphasis added) says, "To him who overcomes, I will give the right to sit *with me* on my throne, just as I overcame and sat down *with my father* on His throne." How can you sit down *with* someone when that someone is *you*?

Consider this also from a logical perspective. Jesus was led into the wilderness to be tempted by the devil.[20] If Jesus and God the Father were the same single individual (not two distinct persons) then the devil would be trying to tempt God the Father, not just Jesus. Did Satan think he could tempt his own Creator? I don't think so. Satan considered Jesus a vulnerable person, not God the Father. Jesus answered, "Worship the Lord your God, and serve Him only."

Speaking of the end-time, Jesus said no one knows the hour or the day, not the angels in heaven, not even the Son, but only the Father.[21] If Jesus and God the Father are one in the same person how did He hide this knowledge from Himself?

Jesus promised the disciples that His *Father* would give them the Counselor (Spirit of truth) to be with them forever.[22]

Jesus is called the "firstborn from the dead."[23] He was crucified on the cross and died for us. He actually died! God the Father is eternal[24] and cannot die.

There are numerous places throughout the Bible that refer to Jesus Christ and the Father as two distinct persons who relate to each other. Possibly the most important, and most powerful example is when Jesus was on the cross. He cried out, "My God, my God, why have you forsaken me?"[25] And "*Father, into your hands I commit my*

---

20 Matthew 4:1–10.

21 Matthew 24:36.

22 John 14:15.

23 Revelation 1:5.

24 Deuteronomy 33:27.

25 Matthew 27:46.

spirit"[26] (emphasis added). Does it make sense that He would call out to someone else if He were that same someone else?

I don't need to quote it here, but I recommend you stop for a moment, read Hebrews 2:9–18, and see what conclusions you come to. It is in the appendix for your convenience.

Let's see if I can put this into perspective by jumping to the end of the story for a moment. Since we are to become God's family, His eternal companions, and we are to love Him and live with Him forever, we will continue to be distinct beings or persons. While we came from God, we are separate in the sense that we have free will, individual personalities and reasoning power, and the ability to live and experience life, and be self-aware on a godly level.

We will never be equal to God (He has existed forever and will continue to exist forever), we will not be as perfect as God (He has been perfect for all eternity and we will have come from a sinful background), and we will never have all the power and authority of God because He created us and we exist by His will, but we will be gods.[27] We are called "children of God" in many verses of the Bible.[28]

Before the physical creation, the Word was with God and the Word was God (divine)[29] but I believe when Jesus Christ was born, the Word became a new creation. Jesus is called the firstborn, our older brother, the Son of God, and many other titles. How can He be our older brother if He is the same single person of God (the Father) who created us? God will always be our Creator/Father and Jesus will always be our older brother.

Everything that the "Word" was is now embodied in the *person* of Jesus Christ. He is our older brother, and we are to live up to His example much like a firstborn child should set a proper example for his/her younger siblings.

Jesus is genetically identical to God. He is a carbon copy, or

---

[26] Luke 23:46.

[27] John 10:34–38.

[28] 1 John 3:1–3.

[29] John 1:1.

clone, of God the Father. They are One. Everything God stands for, Jesus stands for. Everything God believes, Jesus believes. Everything God desires, Jesus desires. Everything God has said, Jesus is! Jesus is an exact spiritual duplicate, or clone, of God.

Jesus said, "… He who has seen Me has seen the Father; so how can you say, 'Show us the Father'? Do you not believe that I am in the Father, and the Father in Me? The words that I speak to you I do not speak on My own authority; but the Father who dwells in Me does the works. Believe Me that I am in the Father and the Father in Me …"[30]

Notice Jesus did not say, "I *am* the Father." He very clearly distinguishes between Himself and the Father. Some people say God is both Father and Son and they use an analogy of a man, his father, and his grandfather. In this example the father is both a father (of his son) and a son (of his father). If we use that example with God (the Father), and we call Him *the Son* then who is *His* father?

We are to become clones of Christ. Notice Ephesians 4:13, where it says, "till we all come to the unity of the faith and of the knowledge of the Son of God, to a perfect man, to the measure of the stature of the fullness of Christ;"[31] Notice it does *not* say the fullness of the Father?

The title of this book was really intended to refer to *us*, not Jesus, but the description also helps us understand Jesus. The entire purpose of our lives is to develop the same perfect, righteous character and love that Jesus Christ *and* God the Father share, while we retain our individual personalities. That will make us *one* with both of them.

In science fiction clones are exact copies of their original counterpart but from the time they are "born," so to speak, they begin to have their own individual experiences. They share a common history, but their futures are different.

---

[30] John 14:9–11.

[31] Ephesians 4:13.

We, on the other hand, are developing our own individual experiences and personalities now, but through God's miracle of the Holy Spirit we are to become identical to Jesus in character. We do not give up our own personalities, or our uniqueness, we take on the perfection of perfect character and perfect obedience to the overarching law of love.

While Christ is *one* with God the Father, we are not yet one with either of them. Jesus set an example for us to follow, an example of godly love. He set an example of how to live our lives.

Jesus never sinned! He was perfect from the beginning, however, once He was born into the flesh and blood world we inhabit, He learned about obedience to the law from our perspective.[32] The original Greek words used for *learned* and *obedience* could be translated as *understood* and *submission*. By living a flesh and blood life with mankind, He saw (and better understood on a day-to-day basis) what we go through as we struggle through our existence in a world filled with sin. Jesus, our Savior, can fully understand and empathize with our struggles and trials and temptations.

The apostles wrote volumes about this subject so we could begin to understand, but without the Holy Spirit we do not have a chance of fully understanding on a spiritual level. This is the reason we must repent, be baptized, and *receive the Holy Spirit*. Only then are we able to truly continue our journey toward perfection.

Repentance is another way of saying you're sorry, but it is a much deeper, spiritual sorrow than just apologizing to someone for their hurt feelings. Repentance involves a very deep, soulful recognition of our own personal sins. It brings us to a close relationship with God and gives us a deep sense of gratitude for who He is and what He is doing for us.

Repentance also requires an understanding of exactly what sin is or we would not feel regret for having sinned.

[32] Hebrews 5:7–10.

It is the Holy Spirit that gives us the understanding we need to begin working toward the fullness and perfection of Jesus. Without the Holy Spirit we are simply blindly living our lives here on earth under the shadow of death.[33] Death hangs over us like the sword of Damocles.

33 Psalms 23:4.

PART II

PRE-HISTORY

CHAPTER 2

THE PLAN

HOW DID THIS ALL BEGIN? ALLOW ME TO OFFER SOME SPECULATION here. There is no proof to this speculation, but it makes a lot of sense to me so let's take this journey together.

We accept these truths to be self-evident. In the Beginning God created the heavens and the earth.[34] It does not say how, it only says God did it. Let's call this the foundation of the world.

Before this "foundation" there must have been a time when God concluded that He would create humans. Why?

At some point He decided to build His family.[35] He decided to express His love to children.

How then, could He go about creating us? He needed workers, angels who would eventually oversee and serve us.[36]

How did he create the spirit world? Obviously, we cannot know how, we just know He *did*. But how did He create the physical world? Ah, that may be a different story. Do not panic, I'm not about to start off on some wild ride here and claim secret revelation, I'm just going to offer a theory; a simple theory at that.

---

[34] Genesis 1:1.

[35] Hebrews 2:10–11; Ephesians 3:14–15.

[36] Hebrews 1:14.

I assume you know who Einstein was, the great physicist? You have probably heard of his theory of relativity; $E=MC^2$? This is probably the most famous equation in the world. In case you have forgotten, it can be simply stated as Energy (E) = Mass (M) times the speed of light squared (C^2). In other words, the energy (E) released from an object is equal to the mass (M) of the object times the speed of light squared (C^2). This equation means that energy and mass are interchangeable.

Scientists continue to study this theory and it is much larger than what I am stating but let's just go with this for a moment.

Think back to high school or college algebra. I hated algebra! But I do remember one very important fact about all equations. If you perform the same adjustment to both sides of an equation, then nothing changes. For example, let's take 2 x 4 = 8. If you divide both sides of that equation by 2 then the equation still balances. Two times four divided by two equals 4, and 8 divided by 2 equals 4. Pretty simple stuff.

Let's apply that concept to Einstein's theory. Divide both sides of his equation ($E=MC^2$) by the speed of light squared (C^2). It would then read $E_{,}C^2 = M$. Or in other words, Mass is equal to Energy divided by the speed of light squared.

God is a spirit being. He has consciousness, He has presence, He is energy. In one sense we could describe Him as pure, conscious, energy.

It seems reasonable to believe that God simply converted some of His own energy into mass (the universe). The mass would be equal to the energy He expended, divided by the speed of light squared (C^2). Science may call this the Big Bang, but it doesn't really matter what it is called, it still came from God.[37] When God speaks, creation happens.

Whether it was a Big Bang or a little bang or an instantaneous *snap* of the fingers, it all came from God. My point is simply that

[37] Colossians 1:16–17; Romans 11:36; Ephesians 3:9; Isaiah 44:24.

this should not be a spiritual *life-or-death* issue for Christians. We know God did it, we just may not agree on *how* He did it. Does that mean we can't get along or that we won't be saved? Of course not.

Many scientists, atheists, and evolutionists are bent on proving that God does not exist when it was God who created everything in the beginning. They use theories like the Big Bang to prove that the universe came into being without God when, in fact, the Big Bang is actually God Himself.

Does it make more sense to believe that matter simply "popped" into existence than it does to believe there is a Creator God? Not to me.

Dr. Del Tackett[38] once said (not a direct quote) to "imagine nothing, nothing, nothing, then suddenly, poof, everything!" Does this sound easier to understand than a Creator God? (Dr. Tackett was arguing in favor of God, not against Him.)

Obviously, this is not a provable issue, but it works for me. Why must scientists use science to try and prove God does not exist? Why can't scientists simply assume God exists and go on about proving how He does what He does?

I suspect God created the spirit world knowing that spirit beings would not fill His desire for companionship but that they would assist him in creating children (us) over eons of time. He went to all this trouble to create us because He loved us even before we were born!

Examine Lucifer's downfall.[39] A study of the Bible will reveal that Lucifer took a third of the angels with him when he rebelled against God.[40]

Why would Lucifer rebel against God? Hmmmm. Could it be that Lucifer did not agree with God? Perhaps he thought he knew better than God? Could it be that Lucifer did not love God? I believe God's love for Lucifer has never changed. God loves all His creation,

---

[38] *The Truth Project*, 2006, focusonthefamily.com.

[39] Isaiah 14:12–15.

[40] Jude 1:6.

and He must regret when something becomes bad. It is His will that all things will be reconciled to Him.[41] We can all identify with this. Have you ever made something and not been satisfied with it? You wish it were better or it had turned out differently, but it didn't?

I doubt God wanted rebellious angels, but I believe He knew some of them would rebel because He gave them free will just as He gave us free will. He created them out of necessity because He had to create an environment wherein, we (His created beings) could learn, develop, and make our own decisions regarding our continued existence.

Earth is that environment. The eternal spirit beings (angels) helped carry out the construction and maintenance of the universe and everything in it. You might call them our guardians. They watch over us whether we believe in God or not. Angels are ministering spirits sent to serve those who will inherit salvation.[42]

The angelic rebellion had to be fully anticipated by God. It had to be. He cannot be surprised because He is omniscient and omnipresent. He had to know that some of the angels would rebel and He knew the implications of that. Yet He created them anyway. He counted the cost, as they say, and decided the end justified the means.

In other words, because God gives us free will He knew some of us may ultimately reject Him, but most (hopefully all) would accept Him. Knowing some may be lost by their own choice, it was worth that risk in order to bring perfect children into His family.

[41] Colossians 1:20; Ephesians 1:10.

[42] Hebrews 1:14.

CHAPTER 3

THE LAST FEW WIRES

If you choose to believe the Genesis account as the absolute total and complete story, then how do you explain dinosaurs since they were apparently here first? If the dinosaurs existed contemporaneously with Adam and Eve, and if Adam and Eve were the only two humans at the time, they wouldn't have had much of a chance against the giant meat eaters of the day, would they? And you would think Noah or Moses, or others would have written about them. They should have been on the ark and would have been alive long after the flood. There should have been numerous records of battles between these great beasts and early man.

But if you choose to believe Darwin and his theory of evolution, there are lots of problems there as well. Volumes have been written showing contradictions and scientific arguments with his theory. In fact, if you research it, you will find that Darwin's own words prove his theory fails.

Darwin said, "If it could be demonstrated that any complex organ existed which could not possibly have been formed by numerous, successive, slight modifications, my theory would absolutely break down. But I can find no such case."[43]

---

[43] *On the Origin of Species*, 1860, Charles Darwin, second British edition, page 189.

His statement has become the modern definition of *irreducible complexity.* Darwin did not have the benefit of today's electron microscopes, x-ray machines, etc. The technology to identify the irreducible complexity in nature simply did not exist during his lifetime.

If you wish to research this subject further, I suggest you begin with the amazing flagellum motor. Go to YouTube.com and search for *flagellum.* That will lead you to many other examples of irreducibly complex organs and organisms.

Do not assume that all scientists today agree with the theory of evolution. But many scientists, cosmologists and particle physicists use Darwin, along with their own research, in their attempts to prove God doesn't exist.[44] Renowned scientist Bill Nye argues that evolution is undeniable, and creationism is totally implausible.[45]

In very general and broad terms, many of today's scientists do not believe God had a hand in the creation or ongoing developments of our universe.

On the other hand, there are many scientists who believe in God. Possibly the most prominent is Director of the National Institutes of Health, Francis S. Collins. In 2020 he won the prestigious $1.3 million Templeton Prize which was created in 1972. He wrote, "The God of the Bible is also the God of the genome, He can be worshipped in the cathedral or in the laboratory."[46]

In verse two of chapter one of Genesis it begins to describe the creation of the earth by God in six days. If God could create everything in six days, couldn't He also have created the universe with a Big Bang if He wanted to? And then couldn't He have *re-created* everything on the earth in six days? The real question here

---

[44] Here are two examples: *God: The Failed Hypothesis*, 2008, Victor Stenger, ISBN-13: 978-1591026525; *Brief Answers to Big Questions*, 2018, Stephen Hawking, ISBN-13: 978-1984819192.

[45] *Undeniable: Evolution and the Science of Creation*, 2014, Bill Nye, ISBN-13: 978-1250007135.

[46] *Language of God: A Scientist Presents Evidence for Belief*, 2006, Francis S. Collins.

is does it matter how He did it? Or when He did it? Or how long it took? Of course not.

Somewhere back in time, after God created the heavens and the earth and the dinosaurs and the plants and everything else, I do believe He created humanoid beings, however, I do not believe these beings had the conscious intelligence of a human as we think of it today.

Follow closely here. I do not believe in evolution of the species as taught today. I do not believe we all simply spontaneously evolved from pond scum or that chimpanzees gradually evolved into humans on their own. But I can accept the possibility that specific advancements within species may have been involved in the developmental phase of mankind.

I believe God may have developed the human species over time and through a series of prototypes if you will. In other words, He created many different creatures (birds, snakes, mammals, etc.) including mankind, but none of these creatures had the gift of independent thought and self-determining will as humans do today.

At the risk of offending some (which is not my intent at all) let me put it this way. The animal world does not think like humans think. Sure, they apparently display some of the same types of emotional responses, and some can be trained to mimic humans, but they just are not the same. Consider the example of a dog versus a human.

Something makes a dog a dog and something else makes humans human. There is something that differentiates humans from every other living creature on earth. What is it?

I believe God created humanoid creatures with certain natural instincts or behaviors. Instincts not unlike bird migration or survival instincts or motherly instincts. Let's call these involuntary responses or attributes like breathing and our beating hearts. But these were not self-conscious beings in the same sense we are.

When the time was right God decided to "create" (or I might say re-create) man in His own image. This means God gave man the ability to think and reason on his own. He gave him the self-consciousness and the awareness of his existence in a way that no other creature has. He gave us the *human spirit.*[47]

To put it another way, He connected the last few "wires" of the brain that allowed mankind to fully function as humans in the "image" of God. He gave us self-awareness, the ability to consider our beginning and our end and to make moral judgments.

God created a universe and galaxies and solar systems and planets and earth and all kinds of life on earth, then continued with the development of all these things. He finally came to the point where He "switched" man's brain on. In other words, He gave man a *human* spirit. I believe this is the point where Genesis picks up the story.

Genesis 1:1 says, "In the beginning God created the heavens and the earth." There is much controversy over the next few verses, but some religious scholars believe the next phrase should be something like, "And the earth *became* without form and void." There is a belief that this "became" was the destructive result of an intergalactic battle between God and Satan (Lucifer) and Satan was cast down out of heaven.[48]

According to this theory, God *re-created* living creatures on earth after this destruction. This again is not a critical issue to me. My salvation does not depend upon whether it happened this way or not. What does matter is that God is the Creator of man in His own image.

This scenario allows for the existence of the earth, dinosaurs, cavemen (not in the image of God by definition) and all other created species that could have existed before Genesis. Then after the destruction (which was a result of Lucifer's rebellion) a re-creation occurred. At this so-called second creation, God finished the creation of man in his fullness. This could also explain why the

[47] Zechariah 12:1.

[48] Luke 10:18.

written historical record only goes back to Genesis and the events and people mentioned there, about six thousand years ago.

On the other hand, He could have done everything in six literal days. It doesn't really matter which! Remember, the passage of time for God is not the same as it is for man.[49]

Let's flash-back to God's purpose for a moment. He wanted to create eternal companions (a family) who He could love, who would never rebel, who would agree with Him, who would love Him, who would worship Him, of their own free will.

Adam and Eve did not fit the bill, so to speak. In fact, they failed miserably. If you read the Genesis account you will find that Eve was deceived[50] by a serpent (real, imaginary, fictional story, I don't know), but Adam willfully sinned against God. Eve was essentially tricked into believing the fruit of the tree of knowledge was good to eat after God had said they would die if they ate of that particular tree. Did the serpent eat the fruit in front of her to "show" her it was good? No one knows how she was deceived but she was.

After Eve ate the fruit, she gave it to Adam and he also ate, but the difference was that Adam knew better. Adam still believed it was wrong to eat and he ate anyway. This is a major difference. One is an innocent but deceived act, the other is willful disobedience.

Unfortunately, the result is the same.[51] Sin is sin, rebellion is rebellion, regardless of the reason. For God there is no excuse for disobedience.

But did God know they would sin? Absolutely! While He had given Adam and Eve a godlike consciousness, He did not give them His own Holy Spirit. Nor did He give them full and total knowledge of "life, the universe and everything" (apologies to Douglas Adams).[52]

[49] 2 Peter 3:8; Psalms 90:4.

[50] 1 Timothy 2:14.

[51] 1 Timothy 2:14.

[52] *Life, the Universe and Everything,* 1995, Douglas Adams, ISBN-13: 978-0345391827, is the title of the third book in the *Hitchhiker's Guide to the Galaxy* science fiction trilogy by British writer Douglas Adams.

Adam and Eve were destined to sin. They had no willpower. They had free will, but they did not have the ability to resist the temptation, nor did they have historical background data, or education, that would have allowed them to make an intelligent, fully informed choice. They had never experienced sin or death.

Do you realize what that means? Adam's sin in the garden of Eden was not an unexpected event. He was predestined to sin because of the circumstances but he was not *forced* to sin. This is a deep concept that we need to examine more closely.

I don't believe in predestined salvation; that involves a free will decision we each must make. However, certain life actions can be predestined without affecting our ultimate free will decisions regarding God.

God created mankind without His spiritual component (the Holy Spirit or Holy Ghost) to *allow* mankind to sin and learn. God gives each of us total free will to make our own decisions so we may experience sin. We will get into that more in the next chapter. Mankind must go through God's one room schoolhouse (life on earth) to develop.

No one has ever been able to live a perfect, Godly life because no one has ever been created fully endowed from birth with God's Spirit, except Jesus Christ!

CHAPTER 4

WHY?

Couldn't God have simply snapped His fingers and we would be perfect? Isn't there another way to create a perfect God family?

Those of you who have children should be able to understand this. Every child tests his or her limits at some point in time. Until we know the boundaries of our individual freedoms, we have no limits. When a child wants something and a parent says, "No" what is the child's response? Generally, it is rebellion. It may be demonstrated visibly, or it may not, but it is rebellion just the same.

Do you remember your childhood? Do you remember being told, "No, you can't have that" and feeling hurt or angry or confused? Have you ever witnessed a young child's temper tantrum in a supermarket? Supermarkets are a great place to study human nature if you pay attention.

Watch people with children as you walk through the aisles or as you stand in the checkout line. I do not mean for the purpose of judging the parent or the child, just watch what happens. You can see the consciousness of the child working. You can almost see their thoughts. Their attention span swiftly jumps from one desirable thing to another, and you can see their outrage at being denied.

Sometimes you can almost *see* their thoughts of, "How dare you refuse Me? I deserve that! I have a *right* to have that!"

You might say that rebellion is unavoidable. It is a necessary evil. The process of growing up from an infant to a child to an adult involves learning the differences between right and wrong. Learning our limitations. Learning to appreciate the needs of others.

We are all human. Rebellion is a large part of life itself. We could carry this discussion on for ages and never really accomplish anything, but I do feel we all have a basic understanding of how the learning process develops in children.

God knew some of His created spirit beings (the angels) would eventually disagree with Him in some way. He also knew that His future family, you, and I, would need to progress though a learning process that would lead to a full understanding of what it means to love and live for all eternity with God.

I am a big science fiction fan. I really enjoy stretching my mind with possibilities of what could be, in space and time, so let's briefly consider the lowly robot.

Would you really want to build a robot as your child or your spouse if you could? Would you want someone who always did exactly what you demanded, when you demanded, how you demanded, but from their programming, not out of love for you? That would not be a true companion. That would be a perfect servant.

On the other hand, would you want someone who never did what pleased you? Someone with whom you couldn't really get along? That would also not be a true loving companion. That would ultimately be an enemy.

Wouldn't you want an *ideal* spouse? Someone whose life would be in harmony with yours. Someone who could think on their own, who had free will, their own personality, but who shared your interests. Someone who loved you. Someone who would never argue with you, not because they couldn't but because they never really disagreed with you. In other words, someone who would truly love you *voluntarily.*

If either party in a marriage is self-focused to the exclusion of their partner's interests, the marriage is doomed to failure. If either party is power obsessed, or controlling over their partner, that marriage is also doomed. A successful marriage requires both parties to be focused on the needs, desires, and well-being of their partner. Too many people are so focused on their own desires, to the exclusion of their partner, that their marriages fail.

This is why almost fifty percent of all marriages in the United States end in divorce or separation.[53] The divorce rate for subsequent marriages is even higher.

We cannot force someone to love us. We cannot force someone to hold a certain belief. We can mandate action, but we cannot mandate attitude. Take our laws for example.

The world is filled with more laws than you can number. There are laws for or against virtually every act imaginable. In some places there are laws making it illegal to kiss in public. What is wrong with kissing in public? *Someone* thinks there is something wrong with it and they passed a law against it.

In the United States the most common highway speed limit is 70 or 75 miles per hour. On the Autobahn in Germany there is no speed limit. Is that fair? No, it is simply the law. Do you always obey the speed limit? Probably not.

If you speed, and you get caught, you pay a fine, but then you probably go right back to your habit of speeding when you think you can get away with it.

Do you agree with all of man's laws? Probably not. Would you obey them all? Unless you are willing to pay a fine or spend time in jail you really do not have a choice. Does the possibility that we would obey every law mean we agree with them all? Does the fact that we might obey them mean we would be a suitable companion to the individual(s) who passed a law to which we object? Of course not.

If their ideas and our ideas do not match, what would it be like

[53] "Divorce Statistics and Facts," wf-lawyers.com.

spending all eternity together? If we were not compatible in our deep beliefs how could we enjoy being with each other forever?

Unfortunately, too many of us find ourselves in marriages or in relationships with other family members with whom we cannot get along. We find that we just do not share the same dreams, the same goals, the same ideals as our companions. This is one reason why there are so many broken marriages and dysfunctional families.

The real underlying cause is our own selfishness but that is another part of the story that we'll get to later.

How would *you* create perfect companions to share all eternity with you? You couldn't simply create a robot. You couldn't create a being that had to be forced to love you. You couldn't create a being that must be constantly, eternally, subject to laws (like no kissing) because there would be laws they would not agree with or accept.

Creating a perfect companion takes time. Lots of time. In God's case, an infinitely long amount of time. If nothing exists, then everything must be created, beginning with the universe. God exists outside our universe. He couldn't have created something bigger than Himself of which He is a part. He didn't create Himself; He is eternal.

The depths of God's plan are beyond our very comprehension because of the physical limitations of our minds which are within the universe.

Consider some Biblical facts:

Jesus' life, ministry, suffering, crucifixion, and death were all planned before the universe was even created. Jesus was the Lamb slain before the foundation of the world.[54] That means His life and death here on earth were planned long before we were created. Think about that for a moment.

God also chose us, individually, to be his children even before the world was created.[55] He forms each of us in the womb.[56]

---

[54] Revelation 13:8; 1 Peter 1:20.

[55] Ephesians 1:4–5; James 1:18.

[56] Isaiah 44:2.

He specifically designed Adam and Eve and chose to place them in the Garden of Eden.

Paul says Eve was deceived but Adam sinned. All (humans) have sinned[57] and the wages of sin is death.[58] It is *appointed* unto man once to die.[59]

The Spirit of God was not freely available to mankind until after Jesus' death. There are numerous Old Testament examples of the Holy Spirit being involved with people, but the purpose was completely different from that of the New Testament.

In the Old Testament the Spirit came *upon* men[60] and caused them to prophesy, to have strength, courage, wisdom, understanding, to become great leaders, etc. Sometimes these benefits were temporary. In other words, the presence of the Spirit could be revoked.

I would not presume to say that God *never* gave the Holy Spirit to individuals in the Old Testament because there are a few special circumstances where the Old Testament refers to the Spirit being *in* a person, but they are few and far between.[61] All I am saying is the Holy Spirit was not openly available to everyone in the Old Testament as today.

Jesus said the Counselor (or Holy Spirit) would not come to the disciples unless He (Jesus) went away.[62] This seems to clearly support the position that the Spirit was not universally available prior to His departure, i.e., the Old Testament.

On the other hand, in the New Testament the Spirit was an indwelling Spirit,[63] or comforter. There is a huge difference between the Spirit being *on* someone and the Spirit *living in* someone. That

[57] Romans 3:23; 1 John 1:8–10.

[58] Romans 6:23.

[59] Hebrews 9:27.

[60] Genesis 41:38; Numbers 11:25; Numbers 27:18; Judges 3:10; 1 Samuel 10:9–10; Micah 3:8; 2 Peter 1:21, etc.

[61] Genesis 41:38; Numbers 27:18.

[62] John 14:25; John 15:26; John 16:7.

[63] Romans 8:9–11; 2 Corinthians 6:16.

difference exemplifies the distinction between the Old Covenant and the New Covenant.[64]

The Holy Spirit was made openly available to all humanity (upon individual conversion) on Pentecost after Jesus' resurrection.[65] Why is this significant? Because that means Adam was created with a human spirit, but he didn't have God's Holy Spirit.

Without the Holy Spirit we cannot understand the things of God.[66] Carnal humans, without God's Spirit are incapable of understanding spiritual things. This means Adam and Eve, without God's Spirit, were incapable of truly understanding God or the concept of sin.

Fortunately, there was *already* a plan in motion! Jesus' life and death had already been laid out on the drawing board so to speak, because God knew Adam would not be capable of living a perfect, righteous life. Since Adam didn't have God's Spirit he couldn't understand and obey God's law.

It might help to think of it this way. Adam was a child. He couldn't understand the things of adults. Consider an ordinary child of, let's say, one year in age. Can you have a normal adult conversation with him about life, careers, love, laws, etc.? Of course not.

Could you expect that one-year-old to take a construction job and help build a house? Certainly not. Similarly, God knew Adam was emotionally and intellectually the equivalent of a one-year-old. Even though he may have been an adult by our standards, by God's standards he was an infant.

Do you really think God was surprised when Adam sinned? Would *you* really be surprised to find your child's hand in the cookie jar, especially if you had set the cookie jar on the floor directly within reach of the child? Do you think God was forced to revert to "Plan B" because Adam failed? Not at all! God knew Adam would sin just as we know a baby is going to mess his diaper.

---

[64] Jeremiah 31:33.

[65] John 15:26; John 16:7; Acts 2:1–4.

[66] 1 Corinthians 2:14.

For a different perspective, let's consider another analogy. I have owned many dogs as pets over the years. They are smart, loyal, reliable companions. I once trained a dog not to eat food that was put down in front of him until I specifically said it was okay to eat it. I could tell him to "Stay," balance a piece of meat on his nose, and he would not touch it or move until I said so.

Here is the question. If I had put rat poison in a piece of meat and placed it on his nose, then explained that this piece of meat had poison in it, told him not to eat it because he would die if he ate it, would he have obeyed? Certainly, he would have followed his training, but would he have truly understood the concepts of poison and death? No. If I had left the room how long do you think it would have been before he would have broken down and eaten it? A few minutes? Hours? Days? I don't know. But would he eventually have eaten it? Absolutely, of that you can have no doubt. And he would have died.

Since a dog does not have the spirit of man, the thing that makes us human, he cannot understand the things we understand. A dog can't understand the concepts of poison or death as we do. It is the same way with us and God. We cannot understand God's existence until we have His Spirit within us.

God is not surprised by anything we do. He can be pleased or unhappy about what we do, but He is not surprised.

God has predestined our overall experience as human beings for our education, but not necessarily our specific day-to-day lives, i.e., our choices. He has given us free will to make decisions, but He controls the circumstances of our lives which affect our decisions. He continually guides our journeys.[67]

Think of it this way. If you were to go on an ocean cruise, let's say from New York to England, you would have lots of free time with lots of daily decisions to make. For example, you could choose when to get up in the morning, when to go to bed at night, what

[67] Psalm 23:3.

time to eat, what to eat, what activities to do, etc. You could even decide to jump overboard and end your voyage, but it wouldn't end the voyage for everyone else.

However, you would have no control over how fast the ship travelled, which route it took, or what day and time it arrived. Other people are in control of those things.

You might say you would have free will to make all your own decisions, but there are other factors that may influence your decisions. The captain could choose to change or cancel a mealtime. He may determine which onboard activities are available at any given time. He might schedule a surprise emergency drill for the middle of the night. He could also detour the ship due to weather.

In other words, you would still have free will, but the outcome could be limited due to reasons beyond your control. The fact that the ship will ultimately dock in England doesn't change.

That is a lot like life. God controls our overall lives, but we have lots of individual decisions to make. He can cause things to happen that will either benefit us, or ultimately be a bad influence for us, and we make choices based upon those changed events. He determines more aspects of our lives than most people realize.[68]

A very wise man, whom I highly respect, named Ravi Zacharias (recently deceased, look him up on YouTube), once said something that, if I remember correctly, goes like this; "God gives us free will to make choices, but He does not give us the right to change the consequences of those choices."

God already knows the outcome of our choices, and He can alter circumstances to sway our decisions, whether we listen to Him or not. When we make bad choices, we, or others, suffer the consequences.

This may not be a perfect analogy, but I hope it gets the point across.

---

[68] Acts 17:24–26.

CHAPTER 5

HOW?

I BELIEVE GOD MUST ALLOW HIS CREATION TO EXPERIENCE LIFE without Him to learn about sin and appreciate His greatness.

Consider this. You probably know what chicken tastes like right? And you probably know what a good steak tastes like right? Well, a chicken had to die so you could know what chicken tastes like. A cow had to die so you could know what steak tastes like.

Jesus Christ had to die so you could know what sin tastes like. Only after you know what sin is, and what it tastes like, can you make an intelligent, informed decision as to whether you like it or not.

Think of your life experiences as a vaccination against a deadly disease.

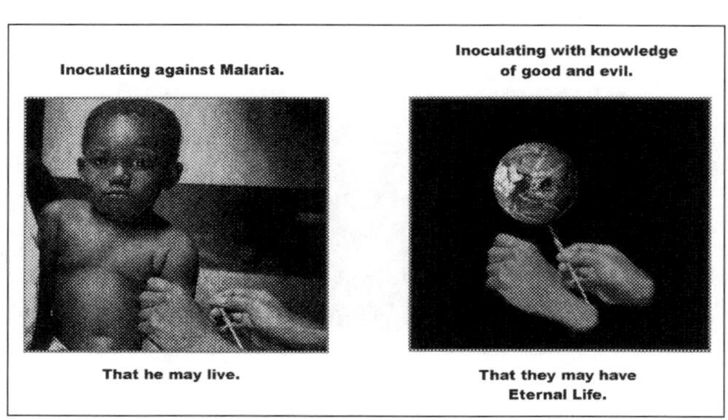

Mankind is in school (earth) to experience sin. And we have the blood of Christ to redeem us from the wages of sin. There is no other way. God will not hold us eternally accountable for a decision based on incomplete data. We must experience law and lawlessness (e.g., good and evil) so we can choose between them with full knowledge and understanding.

You have probably heard of the old "one room schoolhouse" of the early American frontier. In that one room were all the various classes, kindergarten through high school. Imagine being the teacher in that schoolhouse.

At all times you would have to both teach and entertain all the different ages. You must have enough simple learning activities for the youngest children and simultaneously you must stimulate and challenge the oldest children.

Throughout the day many different experiences would be had by all. For example, one child might fall and skin his knee. Another might break a pencil. Another might eat a bad apple and become ill.

Does this mean that each one of their parents intentionally planned each and every event throughout the day? Not at all. But did their parents know the potential for these things to happen? Yes. And were they willing to put their children in this environment for the sake of their education? Absolutely.

Some people excel in school, others struggle. Some may seem to be the "teacher's pet" due to their perceived special treatment. Does this mean they are better than the other students? Not at all. They may work harder, show reliable character, and be called upon for special tasks such as passing out materials or collecting test papers. If teachers need assistance, they usually call upon students with good attitudes who can be relied upon. It is the same with God. He calls various people for specific tasks.[69]

I believe God has put us in His own little one room schoolhouse, earth. Just as school has a curriculum or schedule, God has a

[69] 1 Corinthians 12:28–31.

schedule, or timeline, for all worldly events. Things happen when they are supposed to happen.[70] God oversees our entire education, but He also allows time and chance to take their toll.[71]

Children complain that school is not fair. It isn't meant to be fair; it is an education.

People complain that life is not fair. It isn't meant to be fair; it is an education.

Nothing in this life, fair or not, can last forever except our relationship with God. He gave us life; He can take it, and He can give it again. That is why the Bible speaks of our being resurrected from the dead.[72] When we are ultimately resurrected all the things of the past, our pains, sufferings, and sadness, will be forgotten, similar to the way we, as adults, forget the trials of grade school. We will be new spiritual creations through Jesus Christ.

How could we ever come to the knowledge and understanding of good and evil without being exposed to both in this life, while we are still mortal?

Consider again that one-year old child. When you say, "Don't touch that stove, it's hot," do you think the child truly understands the concept of hot? Not unless he has been exposed to something hot before. But once he has experienced his first burned hand he will understand.

It was necessary for God to place all of mankind in an environment containing *both* good and evil so we can be "burned." It was also *necessary* for Him to allow Satan to enter the garden and tempt Eve. Remember, Satan has no authority unless God allows it.[73]

Many people believe mankind is basically good and the "fall of man" changed the world. Others believe mankind is intrinsically

[70] Matthew 8:29; Matthew 26:18; Luke 21:24; Acts 17:24–27; Romans 9:9; 1 Corinthians 4:5; Galatians 4:4; Ephesians 1:10–12; 2 Thessalonians 2:6; 1 Timothy 6:15; Revelation 9:15.

[71] Ecclesiastes 9:11.

[72] 1 Corinthians 15:50–56; 1 Thessalonians 4:13–18.

[73] Job 1:12; 2:6. These scriptures illustrate that Satan has no authority without God's permission!

evil and that we must be saved. I believe we are born innocent, without sin,[74] but also without God's Spirit. As we develop, we are influenced by Satan.[75]

Satan broadcasts his message to everyone; God also broadcasts His message. Just as physical objects will resonate with sound waves (such as an opera singer breaking a glass), our souls resonate with either God's Holy Spirit or with Satan's spirit. Which broadcast resonates with your spirit?

The Bible teaches that the carnal (man-centered or earthly) mind is enmity towards God and is not capable of being subject to his laws.[76] There was a time when God said that every inclination of the thoughts of man's heart was only evil all the time.[77] This is the natural result of sin. Without God's Spirit mankind will continually deteriorate to the lowest level of self-centeredness because of the ever-present influence of Satan.

As our human spirits develop and grow while we are in human form, we coexist in different stages of development. Some of us are babies, some children, some teens, some adults, and so on. Some of us are well educated, some have no education. Some of us are very scientifically minded, some of us live in remote African or South American tribes.

The fact is, we are all different, but we must eventually come to the same point of spiritual development. It doesn't matter what race, nationality, or sex we are; we must all ultimately learn of God. We must all ultimately decide, with full knowledge and understanding of the consequences of love and sin, whether we wish to spend all eternity with God as part of His loving family or not.

For most of humanity this full understanding and point of decision will come after Jesus Christ returns to earth.[78] Some have

[74] Romans 9:11.

[75] Ephesians 2:2.

[76] Romans 8:7.

[77] Genesis 6:5.

[78] Revelation 20:12–14.

been blessed with the indwelling of the Holy Spirit during our physical existence on earth before Jesus returns.

God had to establish an environment wherein we (His created beings, His eternal family to be) could learn, develop, and make our own decision of continued existence.

Remember the story of Adam and Eve in the Garden of Eden. When the choice was made between the tree of life and the tree of knowledge of good and evil, the plan was confirmed. All humanity was destined to live in a world filled with examples of both good and evil. We were predestined to be exposed to both so we could learn the difference and eventually choose which we prefer.

God loves us so much that He would never force us to live with Him if we don't want to. But life without Him is impossible because He created us. We are a part of Him. He sustains us and gives us each breath.[79] We either choose Him or we choose death.

God said to the ancient Israelites that He was giving them a choice between life and death. He encouraged them to choose life, but it was still their choice![80]

He is always in control, guiding us and teaching us.[81] God does not tempt us,[82] but He will allow us to be tempted. Most importantly, He promises not to allow us to be tempted beyond what we can bear.[83]

In addition to allowing us to be tempted He sometimes authorizes trials.[84]

Consider the story of the exodus from Egypt. God not only sent the Israelites *into* captivity, but He also hardened Pharaoh's heart,[85]

---

79 Job 12:10; Job 33:4; Job 34:14.

80 Deuteronomy 30:19.

81 Isaiah 48:17.

82 James 1:13–14.

83 1 Corinthians 10:13.

84 1 Kings 22:19–23.

85 Romans 9:18.

over and over, and arranged for their release 430 years later, just as He had foretold.[86]

Throughout the Bible there are numerous examples of God prophesying events, and then bringing them about. He has been involved in our lives and education, from the very beginning.

He is in complete control of our lifelong education. We will all be called into account for what we have learned, and how we have lived our lives.[87]

It doesn't matter whether you believe in Him or not, He believes in *YOU.*

[86] Genesis 15:13–16; Genesis 41:25; Exodus 7:3–5; Exodus 9:12; Exodus 10:20; Exodus 10:27; Exodus 11:10; Exodus 12:40; Joshua 24:2–13; Romans 9:17–18.

[87] Revelation 20:12–13.

PART III

THE PRESENT

CHAPTER 6

WHAT IS SIN TODAY?

THAT MAY SOUND LIKE A TRICK QUESTION; "WHAT IS SIN TODAY?" Sin has not changed, but our understanding of sin has changed. People recorded in the Old Testament understood sin as simply breaking one of the Ten Commandments. Many people still believe that today, but sin refers to a much higher law, and our responsibilities of obedience are much higher as well.

Let's take a closer look at this issue that most people, and churches, still do not fully understand. Exactly what is sin? The answer is actually very simple. Sin is the transgression of the law.[88] When you break the law you sin. But the obvious next question is, "What is the law?" That is a more complex issue. That's where people get confused.

The simple answer assumed by most is that the law is the Ten Commandments that were given to Moses and the children of Israel. When you break one of the ten, that is sin; but that is not a complete answer. The commandments were part of a covenant between God and the Children of Israel. Keeping the commandments was

[88] 1 John 3:4.

basically a condition for receiving God's blessings.[89] Breaking the commandments would bring a curse.[90] Nowhere in this covenant or contract does it mention the concept of sin.

Consider this: Is one of the Ten Commandments more important than the others? Surely, if you kill someone it is far worse than if you simply lie about something isn't it? No, it's not.

When asked what the greatest commandment was Jesus said, "You shall love the Lord your God with all your heart, with all your soul, and with all your mind. This is the first and great commandment. And the second is like it: You shall love your neighbor as yourself. On these two commandments hang all the Law and the Prophets."[91]

He could have picked one of the ten, or He could have emphasized that all ten of the commandments were "the law" to be observed but He didn't. He said *love* is the first and great commandment. Well, that's not even listed as one of the ten is it? He said that we are to love God first and love our neighbor second. He went on to explain that all the Law and the Prophets "hang" on these two commandments.

The Ten Commandments give us a list of behavioral requirements. They tell us not to steal, not to kill, not to covet our neighbor's possessions or spouse, etc. They do not teach us to love.

The first four of the ten tell us how we should behave toward God. The last six of the ten tell us how we should behave toward our neighbors. The Ten Commandments do not actually show *love*, they show how we should behave. These are terms of the covenant.

If we could diagram what Jesus said (that all the law and the prophets hang on these two commandments), it would look something like this:

---

[89] Deuteronomy 28:1–14.

[90] Deuteronomy 28:15–68.

[91] Matthew 22:35–40.

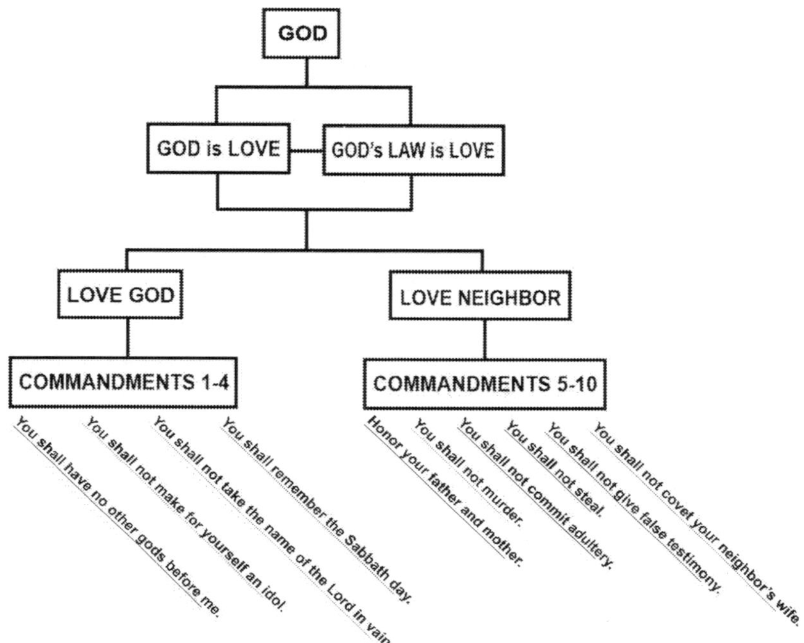

Since carnal man (without God's Spirit) cannot understand the things of God, the Ten Commandments of the Old Testament were designed to be understood by people who were not spiritually minded. They mandate action, not attitude, as a means of explaining to mankind how they should act towards God and one another.

If you truly love someone (by God's definition of love) then your life will be in compliance with the Ten Commandments because they reflect the *result* of love. In other words, if you love someone then you will not kill them, you will not steal from them, you will not commit adultery with their spouse.

Love does no harm to a neighbor; therefore love is the fulfillment of the law.[92] Keeping the Ten Commandments doesn't fulfill the law, it is the *result* of obeying the law of expressing perfect love.

[92] Romans 13:10.

God is love,[93] and He is spirit,[94] which is why we must worship Him in spirit and truth, not with physical commandments of "do this" or "don't do that." The perfect law of God's love produces a change in attitude thereby resulting in changed actions by internal choice, not by mandate. Our minds (thinking) must be transformed.[95]

With superior force you can compel someone to act in a certain way, but no human force can compel someone to *want* to act a certain way. That requires a change of heart. As the old saying goes, "You can lead a horse to water, but you can't make him drink."

I think sin is the most insidious thing in existence, but we get into that in more detail when we define love in the next chapter.

To paraphrase, sin is the transgression of the law, which means sin is willfully failing (or refusing) to express love fully and perfectly.

In the Old Testament the concept of sin was one of "missing the mark." To understand that better let's use the analogy of archery.

The goal in archery is to hit the bullseye with an arrow. Hitting that little red circle in the center of the target (the mark) represents perfection. If we hit anything other than that little red circle, then we have "missed the mark." We are not perfect.

In a spiritual sense, fully expressing spiritual love is the mark we are aiming for. Hitting that mark is perfection, anything else misses the mark. In other words, we sin.

God is perfect and He is molding and shaping us to be His perfect children.[96] Anyone who does not become perfect will eventually die. That is why we are created as mortal beings. We must be exposed to sin so we can "taste it," determine that we don't like it, and learn

---

[93] 1 John 4:8.

[94] John 4:24.

[95] Romans 12:2.

[96] Isaiah 64:8; Jeremiah 18:3–6; Romans 9:20–24.

how to not sin. This is part of our journey toward perfection. Jesus set the standard and shed His blood for us.

Here are a few interesting scriptures on sin and death. They imply that we were predestined to sin, not because we are evil but because it is part of our educational process.

Hebrews 9:27 says,

> It is *appointed* for men to die once, but after this the judgment.

Romans 3:23 says,

> For all have sinned and fall short of the glory of God …

Romans 6:23 says,

> The wages of sin is death, but the gift of God is eternal life in Christ Jesus our Lord.[97]

Ephesians 2:8–10 says,

> For by grace you have been saved through faith, and that not of yourselves; it is the gift of God, not of works, lest anyone should boast. For we are His workmanship, created in Christ Jesus for good works, which God prepared beforehand that we should walk in them.

The goal is for us to learn about God and Christ, to believe in them, to eventually become perfect, and then to live in the God family for all eternity.

Since we now fall under the New Testament, we are not to merely

[97] Romans 6:23.

follow the ten physical commandments of the Old Testament, rather, we are obligated to live under the higher spiritual law of love.[98] One result of perfect obedience to the law of love would be the perfect fulfillment of the Ten Commandments! So, the next question is, what is love and how do we obey it?

[98] John 4:23–24.

CHAPTER 7

EXACTLY WHAT IS LOVE?

How can we express perfect, godly love if we don't know what love is? We tend to get wrapped up in the warm, fuzzy, sentimental "feeling" of the word love. We may think of cozying up with that special someone in front of a fireplace on a cold, winter evening with a nice hot cup of chocolate. That is not the love we're talking about here.

Love is not passive; it is an intentional act. It is very clearly defined in 1 Corinthians 13:4–8 where it says, "Love is patient, love is kind. It does not envy, it does not boast, it is not proud. It is not rude, it is not self-seeking, it is not easily angered, it keeps no record of wrongs. Love does not delight in evil but rejoices with the truth. It always protects, always trusts, always hopes, always perseveres. Love never fails…"

Verse 13 says, "And now these three remain: faith, hope and love. But the greatest of these is love."

The original Greek language uses different words for love, and each has a different meaning. One refers to brotherly love, one to parent/child love, one to husband/wife love, and one refers to godly love. The one listed above in Corinthians is *agape* which refers to spiritual, godly love.[99] These definitions of love are God's definitions, not man's definitions.

It may sound as though love is passive, but these attributes of love take a lot of effort on the part of the person expressing love. Remember the kindness of the Good Samaritan who went out of his way to help a man who had been robbed and beaten?[100] Consider a couple of these attributes along with that story.

Kindness doesn't happen by accident; it takes conscious intent. Kindness means never walking blindly past anyone in need of help. For instance, a person (male or female) carrying packages and walking toward a door may not *ask* for help but a Christian should be aware enough to offer help. Whether or not the person accepts the offer of help is not the issue, a Christian should always offer. That is showing kindness.

Willful failure to express kindness when the opportunity arises is a sin. It means we have missed the mark or the goal of expressing full, perfect love.

And it is more than simply offering help, it's going out of one's way to express acts of kindness. Being nice to others is a fulfillment of the law of love.

What about jaywalking on a city street? The jaywalker is placing his/her own needs above the law and above the interests of all the motorists driving by. This is not expressing love for those drivers. I say this is not just breaking man's law, it is also a sin. Sometimes the result of this sin is instantaneous death as we often see in the news.

Patience is much more than a virtue; it is part of the law! Each time we lose our patience with someone we break the law of love which means we have sinned in the moment.

Boasting is easy, *not* boasting is sometimes difficult. It takes

---

[99] Due to time and space limitations, we will not get into a deep discussion of these definitions here. If you wish to pursue this line of study, I suggest you get a Bible concordance (*Strong's Exhaustive Concordance* is a good choice) from a library or bookstore and research the original Greek definitions.

[100] Luke 10:30–37.

conscious intent to allow others to express their pride in their accomplishments without trying to "show them up" by boasting of our own.

What about rudeness? If you have ever been driving a car when someone cut you off, did you race around and try to cut them off as revenge? That violates several things. It comes from being easily angered, it is rude and it's self-seeking. It is rendering evil for evil. Doesn't quite fit the concept of treating others as you would like to be treated does it?

We must learn to treat people as we would like to be treated regardless of how they treat us.[101] I saw a great saying somewhere that said, "Treat others as if you were the other."

Remember 1 John 3:4 where it says, "Sin is the transgression of the law."[102] This means anyone who does not fully express love, as defined in Corinthians 13, is sinning. We do not have to murder or steal or lie, all we need to do is fail to fully express love and we have sinned. Think about that. Absolutely everyone on earth (except Jesus Christ) has sinned because the law of love is a spiritual law with a spiritual definition that carnal minded mankind (without God's Spirit) does not understand. Even if we could understand we're incapable of total, perfect obedience!

We tend to think in terms of breaking one of the Ten Commandments as being the definition of sin and if we have not actually broken even one then we think we are "good." The fact is every human being has sinned and fallen short of the glory of God because we can't perfectly express love the way God intends.[103]

What better example of true love can we have than that "God so loved the world that He gave His one and only Son that whoever believes in Him shall not perish but have eternal life."[104] God gave birth to Jesus Christ, watched Him grow, then gave Him over to

---

[101] Matthew 7:12.

[102] 1 John 3:4.

[103] Romans 3:23.

[104] John 3:16.

the authorities of the day to be beaten and crucified. Likewise, Jesus willfully, and voluntarily, submitted Himself to this plan because He loved us (you and me) so much.

One of my all-time favorite movie lines comes from a film called *The Confession*, released back in 1999. It starred Ben Kingsley, Amy Irving, and Alec Baldwin. A very thought-provoking movie. I am certain you can locate it if you wish to watch it.

I'll paraphrase the line this way, "People say it's hard to do the right thing. It's not hard to do the right thing, it's hard to know what the right thing is. And when you know what the right thing is, it's hard not to do the right thing." That is such a deep concept that deserves much more meditative thought than we can give it here.

Allow me to rewrite that line relative to love. "People say it's hard to love. It's not hard to love, it's hard to know what love is and how to express it. And when you know what love is and how to express it, it's hard not to love."

The type of love God expresses toward us, the type He wants us to express each other, is a spiritual concept that can be difficult to understand. The best written explanation I know is a short essay on 1 Corinthians 13 written by Henry Drummond back in the late 1800s. The title is, *Love –The Greatest Thing in the World.*[105] You can find various printings of it with a quick Google search. Sometimes it is included in books with some of his other writings.

I cannot recommend this work by Mr. Drummond highly enough. I wish I could simply copy it here, but copyright laws would prevent that. Allow me to quote one paragraph.

When referring to Chapter 13:13, Mr. Drummond says,

> Why is love greater than faith? Because the end is greater than the means. And why is it greater than charity? Because the whole is greater than the part. Love is greater than faith, because the end is greater

[105] *Love: The Greatest Thing in the World*, 2019, Henry Drummond, ISBN-13: 978-1948696029.

> than the means. What is the use of having faith? It is to connect the soul with God. And what is the object of connecting man with God? That he may become like God. But God is love. Hence Faith, the means, is in order to love, the end. Love, therefore, obviously is greater than faith. It is greater than charity again because the whole is greater than a part. Charity is only a little bit of love one of the innumerable avenues of love, and there may even be, and there is a great deal of charity without love. It is a very easy thing to toss a copper to a beggar on the street; it is generally an easier thing than not to do it.

If you take the time to locate a copy of this essay you will never regret it. It offers so much upon which to meditate.

When we love one another, the way God intends, we fulfill the law.[106] And when we know the good we ought to do, and don't do it, we sin.[107]

When we as Christians fully understand love the way God wants us to understand, it becomes easy to express it. When we consciously fail to express love our own conscience convicts us internally and we begin to repent on the spot. This is a step-by-step process toward the fullness and perfection of Jesus Christ.

Just as important as expressing love to all, we must also accept expressions of love in our lives. If we don't allow others to express their love through their kindness, then we deprive them of the blessings God gives to those who obey His law. But that is a discussion for another time.

You may want to consider purchasing a Topical Bible for yourself to study the subject of love and any other subjects that may interest you. As you read, realize it is God speaking to you through His word!

[106] Romans 13:8.

[107] James 4:17.

CHAPTER 8

HOW TO UNDERSTAND THE BIBLE

BEFORE WE GET TO A DEEPER DISCUSSION OF JESUS (AND THE clone), let's take a quick overview look at the Bible. What is the purpose of the Bible? Many people are confused by the size and scope of the Bible. They think it is too difficult to fully understand. Some people think it is just a collection of bedtime stories and fables.

The Bible can be thought of as many different things: An owner's manual for mankind, a story of our history, a love letter from God reassuring us of who we are and why we were created, a roadmap to direct us to our Creator. It contains history, admonition, poetry, allegories, analogies, hyperboles, similes, and interesting stories. It does *not* contain any contradictions, although sometimes there appear to be a few. Every apparent contradiction has a simple explanation if you study it with an open mind.

When you look at the Bible as a complete package and read everything in context with the writing, the cultural timelines and different authors' perspectives, apparent contradictions are easily explained.

In general terms, it is a book to help us understand the meaning of our lives, and our intended relationship to our Creator God. It is the most widely published book in the history of the world, and often the most misunderstood book. To some it is a collection of disconnected books and themes containing some good moral instruction.

In one part it seems to tell us to do one thing and in another it appears to tell us to do something completely different. How are we to make sense of such a confusing book as the Bible?

We must remember that some of what is recorded in the Bible is simply the record of individual life experiences and choices made by those individuals. Some of it is the spoken word of God. All of it is "God breathed," meaning it is exactly what God wanted recorded for our education. We learn from both good and bad examples, don't we? It is always best to learn from the experiences of others rather than making all the mistakes on our own.

Look at it this way. There are two primary sections: The Old Testament and the New Testament. Here is how they fit together.

The Old Testament is a historical record of the early history of man (created in God's image as being self-aware and self-conscious) and how he lived. It includes an overview of how God communicated with early mankind and how He watched over them and guided their lives. It also contains a substantial amount of prophecy but don't worry about prophecy yet. Think of Old Testament prophecy as our future history. That is a study for a future date.

Most importantly, the Old Testament is a record of how God relates to mankind who cannot fully understand nor love God without His Holy Spirit. It records how people treated each other (mostly very poorly), and it is full of examples of how God predicted events, then how He brought those events about.

Throughout the Old Testament, God communicated with mankind in very basic, physical ways because the sinful mind (or carnal mind, or a mind simply focused on things of the flesh instead of spiritual things) is not subject to God's law and is not capable of being subject to it.[108] God's commands were concerned with mandating actions, not attitudes, e.g., do not murder, do not steal, do not commit adultery, etc.

The name "Old Testament," or "Old Covenant," refers to the covenant God made with the Israelites at Mount Sinai after He had freed them from slavery in Egypt. Today, the Jewish people still live by the contractual obligations (Ten Commandments) of the covenant that was ratified at mount Sinai.

I highly recommend a book on this subject by Rabbi Jacob Neusner entitled, *A Rabbi Talks with Jesus*.[109] It is an imaginary, but fact-based discussion between Rabbi Neusner and Jesus with dialog taken directly from the book of Matthew. It clarifies many differences between Christianity and Judaism in a very easy to read style.

If you're a history buff and you want to learn about most of the famous people of the Bible and the genealogy and history of Israel, then read the Old Testament.

The New Testament, on the other hand, is completely different but we must first understand a very important point. The New Testament (or New Covenant) begins in Old Testament times. Just because we turn the page from Malachi (Old Testament) to Matthew (New Testament) doesn't mean the times were different. The society, culture, and customs were the same as those we read about in the Old Testament. Jesus Christ was born and grew up under the Old Covenant laws.

The people, even the religious sects, still did not have God's Holy Spirit so God dealt with them in many ways as you would deal with a child.

The New Testament is called "New" because it describes the details of a New Covenant between Christ and humanity. The focus

---

108 Romans 8:7.

109 *A Rabbi Talks with Jesus*, 2000, Rabbi Jacob Neusner, ISBN-13: 978-0773520462.

shifts from one of physical obedience, justice, customs, national identity, etc., to one of God's love. This new contract, or testament, took effect upon Christ's death, not while He was alive.

Having said that, how does one understand the New Testament? Matthew, Mark, Luke, and John (referred to as The Gospels) contain the historical record of the birth, life, and death of Jesus Christ. The Gospels tell us where Jesus went, what He did, who He spoke to, what He said, what happened to Him, etc.

The book of Acts is a historical record of the travels and teachings of the apostles after Christ's resurrection. The book of Acts and the four Gospels were written as personal, eye-witness accounts.

The books of Romans through Jude are primarily letters written by Paul the apostle and a couple of others. They are letters written to specific church locations or individuals, and they contain instruction on how we should live and grow as Christians.

The book of Revelation is filled with prophecies of future events. Some of these events have already occurred but many are yet to come.

To understand who Jesus was, where He lived, what He did, and what He said, read through Matthew, Mark, Luke, and John. To understand what the apostles said, and where they traveled after Jesus' death, read the book of Acts. But to really understand what Jesus meant, what His message was, how to be a Christian, read the letters of the apostles (particularly the letters of Paul) who devoted their entire lives to preaching the gospel and expounding upon Jesus' message. Paul was the most prolific writer, so his explanations tend to be much more thorough and clearer.

Now consider this; Throughout Matthew, Mark, Luke, and John there are many stories of the parables Jesus spoke and the miracles He performed.

Imagine being one of His disciples at that time. You would think you would have a pretty good understanding of what He was teaching wouldn't you? I mean, if you ate, drank, slept, and walked with Him for three and a half years you would have an "inside connection" and you should understand everything He stood for. His message would be crystal clear, right?

But as you read The Gospels you will find Jesus repeatedly asking his disciples, "Do you still not understand?"[110] No matter how many parables they heard, or how many miracles they witnessed, or how much time they spent in discussion with Him, they never quite understood what He was talking about.

The very disciples who spent over three years with Him never fully understood Him. Remember, at that time they still had not received the Holy Spirit[111] so they were unable to understand spiritual things. If *they* could not understand Him, how could the rest of the world possibly have understood Him?

Once the disciples asked Him why He spoke in parables.[112] His answer? Because the knowledge of the secrets of the kingdom of heaven had not been given to the people. Even with all their time together, it was not until after His resurrection that Jesus, "opened their understanding, that they might comprehend the Scriptures."[113]

None of the disciples had the Holy Spirit while they were with Him. The Spirit was *with* them, but it did not become available to dwell *within* them (or mankind) until the day of Pentecost after Jesus' crucifixion and resurrection.

After He opened their understanding, and after they received the Holy Spirit on Pentecost,[114] the disciples (then called apostles) began to travel and preach about Him and His message. It is in those writings that we begin to understand the mind and heart of Jesus.

From that time forward those who repent, are baptized, and receive the Holy Spirit, can begin to understand God. Some people have the Holy Spirit now and some do not. This means some people

---

110 Matthew 16:8–9; Mark 8:21; Mark 9:32; Luke 9:45.

111 John 16:13; Acts 2:1–4.

112 Matthew 13:10–15; Mark 4:10–13.

113 Luke 24:45.

114 Acts 2:1–4.

understand the Bible a little differently from the average person on the street.

As in the little red schoolhouse, we are all at different levels of development. Because of this we often argue over scripture.

What purpose does all our arguing serve? Take the issue of our going to heaven as an example. Some believe those who have died are already in heaven. Some do not. Exactly what does the Bible say?

The Old Testament says, "For the living know that they will die; but the dead know nothing, and they have no more reward ..."[115] If the dead in the Old Testament had gone to heaven this scripture would not make sense.

Jesus said, "No one has ever gone into heaven except the one who came from heaven – the Son of Man."[116] That's pretty clear language to me.

In the book of Acts, Peter said, "For David did not ascend to heaven ..."[117] David was a man after God's own heart.[118] If he didn't go to heaven how could anyone else have gone?

The book of Revelation speaks of a *first* resurrection.[119] How could anyone have gone to heaven before the *first* resurrection that is mentioned as a future event in Revelation?

It seems clear that no one entered heaven before Jesus but did all the dead in Christ suddenly begin to enter heaven upon their death or are they simply asleep and awaiting the resurrection?[120]

A very well-known scripture that seems to support going to heaven is Luke 23:43, where Jesus said to the thief on the cross, "I tell you the truth, today you will be with me in paradise." This seems to contradict everything I said above doesn't it? The explanation is very simple but twofold.

---

[115] Ecclesiastes 9:5.

[116] John 3:13.

[117] Acts 2:34.

[118] 1 Samuel 13:14; Acts 13:22.

[119] Revelation 20:4–6.

[120] 1 Thessalonians 4:13–18.

First, the original Greek word used for paradise is "*paradeisos*" which means an Eden, or a place of future happiness. Paradeisos is only used four times in the Bible. The Greek word for heaven is "*ouranos*" which refers to heaven as the abode of God. Luke was referring to the thief's future life in God's kingdom, wherever that may be.

Second, the original Greek language used in the Bible did not have punctuation marks. The original King James translators put all the punctuation marks (throughout the New Testament) where they felt they would be most appropriate. Since the translators probably believed they would go to heaven upon death, they placed a comma between the words truth and today. Clearly this contradicts all the other scriptures in the Bible.

The fact is the comma should be placed between the words *today* and *you*. The scripture would then read, "I tell you the truth today, you will be with me in paradise." Jesus judged the thief's repentant attitude, and belief in Him, as being sufficient for salvation. He was simply stating that the thief would be saved (enter the kingdom of God), not that he would go to heaven that very day.

This understanding solves the apparent contradiction, so this scripture agrees with all the other heaven related scriptures.

But is that an issue that we, as Christians, should argue and dispute about, whether people have already gone to heaven or not? Is it an issue that will determine our eternal salvation? No. To me it is clear that no one has gone to heaven yet. You may believe otherwise. We don't need to argue about it. I am not here to preach that you are going to hell if you don't believe what I do. We will learn the truth in due time.

Many people believe we have an immortal soul. That is also not what the Bible teaches. It clearly states the soul that sins shall die.[121] Jesus said to be afraid of the One who can destroy both soul and

[121] Ezekiel 18:4.

body.[122] And no, I do not believe you're going to go to hell and *burn forever*. There are so many scriptures that support my position, but I will only give you two references for now.

Perhaps the single most quoted scripture in all history is John 3:16, where it says, "For God so loved the world that He gave His one and only Son, that whoever believes in Him shall not perish but have eternal life."

Most people read that quickly and just gloss over it, focusing on the fact that God gave His only Son. But focus on the last seven words, "*shall not perish* but have eternal life" (emphasis added). Let this sink in for a moment. There are only two options here, perish or eternal life. Both options are not offered together. Perishing does not mean living forever in hell. In order to be tormented for all eternity in a burning hell we would have to have eternal life, which we do not receive unless we believe in and accept Christ as our savior!

The original Greek word translated to "perish" is "*apollumi,*" which means to be destroyed. Without Christ the wicked will be destroyed. They will cease to exist.[123]

There will come a time when the incorrigibly wicked will have to be "put down" just as a ravenous, rabies infected animal must be put down. You cannot keep a rabid dog as a pet, it would be dangerous to everyone and it would also suffer until it died. The same is true of those who refuse to accept Jesus Christ and learn to love.

Consider this from a different perspective. God loves you so much that if you don't do exactly as He says, He will torment your soul for all eternity in the fires of hell. Does that sound like a loving God? No! But that is exactly what most religions today teach. They simply don't understand the immeasurable depth of God's love for all of humanity.

Accepting Jesus Christ as your savior is the only way to eternal life in God's kingdom.

---

[122] Matthew 10:28.

[123] Revelation 21:8.

The next scripture I want you to see is in Timothy.[124] It says the King of kings and Lord of lords alone is immortal. If that scripture is true, how could you and I have an immortal soul? That scripture *must* be true, or we can just throw the entire Bible out the window!

It is my belief that the entire concept of eternal torment in the fires of hell is a Satan inspired concept designed to control people through fear. This concept gained popular acceptance after the publication of Dante Alighieri's *The Divine Comedy* in the year 1320,[125] and it conforms to a large part of Catholic doctrine.

Many people (so-called Christians) delight in arguing over what they believe (what they have been taught) rather than trying to understand what the Bible says.

I met a man once who spent endless hours arguing with anyone who would listen, about the exact definition of the word "amen" used throughout the Bible. He claimed he had superior knowledge that everyone was using the word incorrectly, and that they didn't understand what they were saying, but he had no biblical references to support his argument. I chose not to spend much time with this individual.

Instead of arguing with each other over trivial matters, we should be encouraging each other in sincere love.[126] We should strive to prove all things to ourselves,[127] learn to love, and leave the rest to God.

124 1 Timothy 6:15–16.

125 Many different printings are available. One is, *The Divine Comedy*, 2016, Dante Alighieri, ISBN-13: 978-1420951660.

126 Romans 12:9–21.

127 1 Thessalonians 5:21.

CHAPTER 9

WHAT NOW?

FACE IT, WE ARE ALL GOING TO DIE. THAT IS ALL WE KNOW FOR certain. Except for Jesus Christ (and modern immediate medical resuscitation which isn't truly death), no one has ever returned from the dead to explain the truth of what happens after we die.

No one has the power to prevent death or to reincarnate themselves. We did not bring ourselves into existence and we don't have the power to *save* ourselves or anyone else, so when it's over, it's over. It does not matter how good we are in this life. Jesus Christ is the only one who claims to be the *only* way to eternal life. He says we cannot earn salvation by good works,[128] but He offers it to us as a free gift if we will believe in Him, stop sinning, and learn to love.

In today's world most people don't see themselves as sinners. People say they try to do the right thing, and they think they are pretty good, so they don't believe God would send them to hell. They don't see the need to turn to Jesus, so they don't take the Bible seriously.

The Bible says if we have faith, we can have eternal life, and we

[128] Titus 3:4–8.

must have works to go with our faith,[129] but we cannot earn salvation with our works.[130] Many are confused by this. What do we do now?

The apostle Peter answered that very question in Acts 2:37–39 (emphasis added).

> When the people heard this, they were cut to the heart and said to Peter and the other apostles, Brothers, what shall we do? Peter replied, Repent and be baptized, every one of you, in the name of Jesus Christ for the forgiveness of your sins. And you will receive the *gift* of the Holy Spirit. The promise is for you and your children and for all who are far off – for all whom the Lord our God will call.

Jesus said, "The kingdom of God is near. Repent and believe the good news!"[131] An important step along this road to salvation is repentance. But if we don't first *believe* then we have no perceived need for repentance.

The beginning steps toward eternal life include belief, repentance, being baptized and receiving the Holy Spirit. We must come to a point in our lives where we are truly sorry for things we have done, attitudes we have had, and for ignoring God Himself.

We must come to a point in our lives where we accept (on faith) that God exists, that He created us, that He owns us, and that Jesus Christ is His son. We must submit our entire life to Him. Then we will begin to understand how we have failed to express true spiritual love throughout our lives.

Once we stop living for ourselves, we can truly repent for our past sins. We can then ask Jesus Christ to come into our lives.

For some, repentance can come first, before belief. People can become so frustrated, depressed, and disgusted with the condition

---

129 James 2:26.

130 Ephesians 2:8–9.

131 Mark 1:14.

of their life that they reach repentance first, then turn to God as a last resort. Others may come to a point where they are seeking God without realizing their own sinful condition.

Once we reach either of these points in our lives we need to be baptized. It does not matter who (which Christian denomination) does the baptizing or where it's done. What matters is how it is done. It is important to be baptized in the name of Jesus Christ for the forgiveness of our sins and through laying on of hands we receive the gift of the Holy Spirit.

Different denominations have different beliefs as to how baptism should be done. I believe the biblical method, complete submersion under water. John the Baptist baptized Jesus *in the Jordan river*,[132] and Jesus went up *out of the water*. He wasn't just hit with a few sprinkles.

When Philip baptized the eunuch, it says they both "went *down into the water* and Phillip baptized him. When they came up *out of the water* ..."[133] (emphasis added). Clearly, New Testament apostles followed Jesus' example as well.

It is my belief that we should follow Jesus' example because baptism is symbolic of washing away our past sins. Sprinkling doesn't wash away much but total emersion does.

It is also symbolic of our willingness to submit our lives to God. You might think of it as a sort of initiation ritual. If you're willing to obey and be baptized, then you are serious enough to follow through with changing your life.

I do not believe in baptizing infants because they are not old enough to understand what's happening, much less are they able to fully repent of their sins. A person must be mature enough to understand what all this means, not just undergo a ritual to satisfy their parents, priest, or community. An infant or young child does not yet understand the concept of sin, nor are they able to come to grips with their own sins.

---

[132] Matthew 3:16.

[133] Acts 8:38–39.

There are Old Testament examples where God chose men at least twenty years old to join the army.[134] Perhaps He feels this is an appropriate age of accountability, I don't know, but infants and young children have not yet learned the difference between right and wrong, and they can't be truly sorry for sin according to biblical definition. Godly sorrow brings repentance that leads to salvation and leaves no regret.[135]

True repentance comes from a self-determined desire to submit your life to your Creator God and to dedicate your life to pleasing and worshipping Him. This cannot be forced upon you; it must come from within you. It means giving up your own will and accepting His will in your life.

After we believe God, fully and sincerely repent, get baptized and receive the Holy Spirit, then what? How should we live as Christians? I submit to you there are three specific areas on which we should focus.

First, Love the Lord your God with all your heart,[136] and express gratitude for who He is and what He is doing for us. Re-read the Ten Commandments[137] and remember, the first four focus on worshiping (loving) God while the last six are basically descriptions of how people should live, written specifically for people who did not have the Holy Spirit. These are contractual conditions of the original covenant.

Christians today must rise above these physical rules and learn to worship in spirit and truth. We must develop a loving relationship with, and worshipful attitude toward, God.[138] Open your heart and let Him put His law in your mind and write it on your heart.[139]

---

[134] Numbers 1:2–3.

[135] 2 Corinthians 7:10.

[136] Matthew 22:37.

[137] Exodus 20:3–8.

[138] John 4:23–24.

[139] Jeremiah 31:31–34.

As we learn more about loving God and worshipping Him, we also learn more about gratitude towards Him.

Second, learn the physical attributes of love and focus on them internally. In other words, open yourself to allow God to change you from the inside out. I am certain you have heard the old expression, "You are what you eat." Well, you are also what you think! You are the sum total of every book you read, every movie you watch, every person you meet and every thought you have. Those things make you who you are on the inside. You could lose an arm, or a leg and you would still be the same person with the same consciousness. God will perfect who you are on the inside, but it is impossible to change all that overnight. It takes time.

It is said that our five senses (taste, touch, smell, hearing, seeing) feed information to our brains but our brains are nothing more than dust from the earth. Your senses feed information to your spirit, and your spirit stores the sum total of who you are. This is what the Holy Spirit must work with.

We must change how we think and what we think about. For example, Paul wrote to the Philippians, "Whatever is true, whatever is noble, whatever is right, whatever is pure, whatever is lovely, whatever is admirable – if anything is excellent or praiseworthy – think about such things."[140]

Think about the definition of love as expressed in 1Corinthians 13:4–8. The more we focus on these love attributes the more we will express the fruits of the Spirit; joy, peace, patience, kindness, goodness, faithfulness, gentleness, and self-control.[141]

When we become Christians, we begin a journey down the road to becoming new creations.[142] We are to be made new in our attitudes[143] so it behooves us to work toward that end by better controlling what we think about, how we think and how we act

[140] Philippians 4:8.

[141] Galatians 5:22.

[142] 2 Corinthians 5:17.

[143] Ephesians 4:22–25.

whether with others or alone. This way we can focus on loving and serving our neighbors.

The more we fill our conscious thoughts with God and love, the more we displace the old thoughts that make us who we are now. This is a slow process of becoming who God wants us to be.[144]

Paul wrote to the Galatians that we should live by the Sprit and we will not gratify the desires of the sinful nature. The sinful nature desires what is contrary to the Spirit, and the Spirit what is contrary to the sinful nature. They conflict with each other. The acts of the sinful nature are obvious: sexual immorality, impurity, and debauchery; idolatry and witchcraft; hatred discord, jealousy, fits of rage, selfish ambition, dissensions, factions, and envy; drunkenness, orgies, and the like. Those who live like this will not inherit the kingdom of God. But the fruit of the Spirit is love, joy, peace, patience, kindness, goodness, faithfulness, gentleness, and self-control.[145]

Jesus said we must love one another as He has loved us.[146]
Paul said the only thing that counts is faith expressing itself through love.[147]

We are to clothe ourselves with compassion, kindness, humility, gentleness, and patience. We must learn to be forgiving and put on love which binds all these things together.[148]

> Let us love one another, for love is of God; and everyone who loves is born of God and Knows God. He who does not love does not know God, for God is love. In this the love of God was manifested toward us, that God has sent His only begotten Son into the world, that we might live through Him.[149]

---

[144] Romans 12:2.

[145] Galatians 5:16–23.

[146] John 13:34–35.

[147] Galatians 5:6.

[148] Colossians 3:12–15.

[149] 1 John 4:7–9.

There are many scriptures that show we must learn to love God and one another. Here are a few under this footnote.[150]

Third, we need to learn to pray without ceasing. Many people misunderstand prayer. They think the only time they need to pray to God is when they want something or need help getting out of trouble. They get on their knees and fold their hands because that is what you are *supposed* to do right?

They treat Him more like a genie in a bottle instead of their Creator God. They think they can bargain with God by offering Him something in exchange for answering their prayer. He already owns everything, including YOU!

We all need to stop asking for *stuff*. Look around you at children. They always seem to be begging for something, especially around Christmas time. Of course, there's nothing wrong with children asking for something or needing help but if those were the *only* times they talked to their parents wouldn't that be sad? We tend to be like little children coming to God, always asking for something. Our prayers should not be a long wish list of things we want or need. We should simply talk with God more often.

That is all prayer really is, just talking with God. He is always with us, 24/7. It doesn't matter what we are doing or where we are, He is there with us. If you are driving, He is in the car with you. There is a bumper sticker that says, "God is my co-pilot." It should say He is your *PILOT*!

When God becomes real to you and you accept the fact that He is always with you then you can simply talk to Him. Think of Him as family. He is your Father after all.[151] Would you consider going on a long drive with other family members in the car and never speaking a word to them? How would they feel? How would you feel if you were the passenger in a car and the driver (let's say your spouse) never spoke a word to you?

---

[150] 1 John 4:11–12; 2 John 1:5–6; Romans 13:8–10.

[151] 2 Corinthians 6:18.

You can talk with God any time, any day, all day. When the scripture says to pray continually[152] it means to have a prayerful attitude and to be always in mental communication with God. It means to have an attitude of gratitude toward God for all He has done for you as His child. How often do you simply thank Him for being who He is?

It means to appreciate (and talk with Him about) the beauty and glory of His creation. It means to study His word (the Bible) on a regular basis. It does not matter whether you read it or listen to it on a CD or the internet, it's just important that you study the Bible. When you read His Word, it is the same as Him sitting next to you telling you His thoughts in person.

When you study in this way the Holy Spirit will guide you and expand your understanding in ways you never knew possible.

Remember, all scripture is *God-breathed* and is useful for teaching, rebuking, correcting, and training in righteousness, so that the man of God may be thoroughly equipped for every good work.[153] It does not say that all scripture is *law* but simply that it was *breathed* or *inspired* by God and is useful for our training!

As we have seen, the entire law is summed up in a single command: "Love your neighbor as yourself."[154]

Are we bound to follow all the laws and commandments of the Old Covenant? Do we *earn* salvation by being obedient to all the rules and sacrificial rituals written in the Bible? No.

Ephesians 2:8–9 (emphasis added) says,

> For it is by grace you have been saved through faith – and this not from yourselves, *it is the gift of God* – not by works so that no one can boast. *For we are God's workmanship*, created in Christ Jesus to do good works, *which God prepared in advance for us to do.*

152 1 Thessalonians 5:17.

153 2 Timothy 3:16.

154 Galatians 5:14.

Philippians 2:12–13 (emphasis added) says,

> Therefore, my dear friends, as you have always obeyed – not only in my presence, but how much more in my absence – continue to work out your salvation with fear and trembling, for *it is God who works in you to will and to act according to His good purpose.*

Jesus said He had come to fulfill all the law and the prophets.[155] Upon the death of Jesus (the testator) we come under His will, the New Covenant.[156]

In Romans 7:4 Paul said,

> You also have become dead to the law through the body of Christ …

In verse 6 (Emphasis Added) he said,

> But now we have been delivered from the law, having died to what we were held by, so *that we should serve in the newness of the spirit and not in the oldness of the letter.*

In Galatians 2:16–21 he said,

> Knowing that a man is not justified by the works of the law but by faith in Jesus Christ, even we have believed in Christ Jesus, that we might be justified by faith in Christ and not by the works of the law; for by the works of the law no flesh shall

155 Matthew 5:17.

156 Hebrews 9:15–17.

> be justified … for I through the law died to the law that I might live to God … I do not set aside the grace of God; for if righteousness comes through the law, then Christ died in vain.

And finally, in Ephesians 4:1–3 he said,

> I, therefore, the prisoner of the Lord, beseech you to walk worthy of the calling with which you were called, with all lowliness and gentleness, with longsuffering, bearing with one another in love, endeavoring to keep the unity of the spirit in the bond of peace.

Paul was explaining the *purpose* of the law when he said in Galatians 3:19–25,

> What purpose then does the law serve? It was added because of transgressions … before faith came, we were kept under guard by the law, kept for faith which would afterward be revealed. Therefore, the law was our tutor to bring us to Christ, that we might be justified by faith. But after faith has come, we are no longer under a tutor.

And Jesus said the true worshipers will worship in spirit and truth.[157]

After repentance we are baptized and that is when, with the laying on of hands, we receive the Holy Spirit. Only then can we begin to help mold our lives into the same loving spirit that Jesus Christ showed during His life here on earth. I say we can help because it is not up to us, it is in God's hands. We simply must voluntarily submit to His will and allow Him to work in us through

[157] John 4:23–24.

the Holy Spirit. We learn through both trials and blessings. God disciplines us just as a human father disciplines his son.[158]

When you believe, repent, and get baptized in the name of Jesus and receive the Holy Spirit, you will begin to live a more full and abundant life[159] with confidence in your own salvation.

We were created with a need to be loved. God fills that need and is waiting to shower us with His love for all eternity. What He wants from us now is to act justly, to love mercy and to walk humbly with Him.[160]

Study the complete twelfth chapter of Romans. It discusses an inner transformation of our hearts and minds. It tells us how to act and how to express love in our lives. I have included the entire chapter in the appendix at the end of this book to make it easy for you to find.[161]

> Now all has been heard; here is the conclusion of the matter: Fear God and keep His commandments, for this is the whole duty of man. For God will bring every deed into judgment, including every hidden thing, whether it is good or evil.[162]

Our present sufferings are so minor and temporary compared to what God has in store for us[163] and He is personally overseeing our development so we may rejoice in His kingdom.[164] Jesus is preparing a special place for us so all we need to do is hang on, finish the race, and get there.[165]

The future looks incredibly bright, no matter how dark and

---

158 Hebrew 12:2–11.

159 John 10:10.

160 Micah 6:8.

161 Romans 12:1–21.

162 Ecclesiastes 12:13.

163 Romans 8:18.

164 Romans 8:28.

165 John 14:2–4.

gloomy the world around us appears now. We will live, learn, and love with God our Father and Jesus Christ our older brother for all eternity. What more could we ask?[166]

I can't wait to hear Him say, "These are my beloved children, in whom I am well pleased."[167]

As I said before, the speculations I put forth in the beginning chapters could turn out to be wrong, only God knows for now. But I find the speculative concepts to be very exciting and encouraging. The important thing is they don't really matter where salvation is concerned.

I have not intentionally twisted any of the quoted scriptures (in contradiction to other scriptures) to suit my message. If you feel I have, then prove it to yourself. Research them and find the truth for yourself.

Remember, the only thing that really matters is faith, expressing itself through love.[168] Our salvation does not depend upon speculation. Our salvation depends upon Jesus Christ alone. Everything else will be revealed when He returns.

While we await the return of Jesus Christ, and the world appears to be crumbling around us, we can be at peace because we understand the plan God has for us. When you realize that God is in control you understand that everything, good or evil, has a place in our learning curriculum.[169]

The more good we witness the more joyful we can be that we know the outcome. The more evil we witness the more we detest it, and we know that God will ultimately solve the world's problems.

We can reflect on Jesus' words when He said, "My kingdom is not of this world,"[170] and we can take comfort that our future will also be with Him in His kingdom.

---

166 Revelation 21:1–8.

167 Matthew 3:17.

168 Galatians 5:6.

169 Romans 8:28.

170 John 18:36.

The apostle Paul said to think on things that are true noble, right, pure, lovely, admirable, excellent, and praiseworthy.[171] These positive, uplifting thoughts not only bring us peace and comfort, but they feed our spirits and bring us closer to the perfect, full spiritual likeness of Jesus Christ.

We can't do this by ourselves, God and Jesus make all things possible.[172] It is the work of the Holy Spirit living in us that brings about the changes so that we can become new creations.[173] Jesus Christ died to make eternal life available to all and the Holy Spirit gives us a spirit of strength, not fear.[174] With God as our Father and Jesus Christ as our older brother there is nothing to fear.

One thing I know for certain, my salvation is secure. Is yours?

---

171 Philippians 4:8–9.

172 Matthew 19:26.

173 Ephesians 4:22–24; 4:29–32.

174 2 Timothy 1:7.

PART V

CONCLUSION

CHAPTER 10

FINAL THOUGHTS

I WANT TO LEAVE YOU WITH ONE FINAL ANALOGY TO CONSIDER. A normal woman produces one egg at a time for reproduction. A normal man releases about one billion sperm during sex. All those tiny sperm fight their way to the egg but only *one* will be successful in joining with that egg. When that happens all the rest of the sperm will perish, they have no choice, they have no say in the matter.

That one sperm, and that one egg, contain all the DNA of the man and woman. Those two DNA strands join to become a new creation; a new human being.

On the other hand, God has created billions of humans but just one single Jesus Christ. Not just one of us, but *every* one of us is given the opportunity to join with Christ and become a new creation.[175] Our DNA joins with God's DNA through Jesus so that we can become true children of God for all eternity.

Each of us has the freedom to either accept Jesus or reject Him. Those who accept Him will receive the gift of eternal life. *Only* those who willfully reject Him will perish. God has given *you* the freedom to choose.

---

[175] 1 Corinthians 6:17; 2Corinthians 5:5.

Imagine what His kingdom will be like when everyone, every single being will be perfect in nature, expressing perfect love toward one another. We'll all still have our own individual personalities, in other words you will still be *YOU*, but there will be no crime, no hatred, no death, no sorrow, no sin.

You can *choose* to become a perfect clone of Jesus by choosing life, or you can choose to perish. Those are your only two options, because without God as our sustainer we can't exist, and unless He gives us the gift of eternal life (as He promised through His Son Jesus Christ) we will definitely perish.

This is the beauty of free will. This is the glory of God's love for us. He wants you to choose life. The choice is yours and yours alone.

APPENDIX

THIS APPENDIX CONTAINS A CHRONOLOGICAL LISTING OF SCRIPTURES used throughout this book. A variety of translations are used so if a particular scripture does not exactly match your Bible, check another translation.

These quotes are from the KJV, the NKJV, or the NIV. I chose each version based on my preference of the translation relative to the subject matter.

Genesis 1:1
In the beginning God created the heavens and the earth. (NKJV)

Genesis 1:26–27
Then God said, "Let us make man in Our image, according to Our likeness; let them have dominion over the fish of the sea, over the birds of the air, and over the cattle, over all the earth and over every creeping thing that creeps on the earth." So God created man in His own image, in the image of God He created him; male and female He created them. (NKJV)

Genesis 2:7
And the Lord God formed man of the dust of the ground, and breathed into his nostrils the breath of life; and man became a living being. (NKJV)

Genesis 2:24
Therefore a man shall leave his father and mother and be joined to his wife, and they shall become one flesh. (NKJV)

Genesis 3:19
"By the sweat of your brow you will eat your food until you return to the ground since from it you were taken; for dust you are and to dust you will return." (NIV)

Genesis 6:5–7
The Lord saw how great man's wickedness on the earth had become, and that every inclination of the thoughts of his heart was only evil all the time. The Lord was grieved that He had made man on the earth, and his heart was filled with pain. So the Lord said, "I will wipe mankind, whom I have created from the face of the earth – men and animals and creatures that move along the ground, and birds of the air – for I am grieved the I have made them." (NIV)

Genesis 15:13–16
Then the Lord said to him, "Know for certain that your descendants will be strangers in a country not their own, and they will be enslaved and mistreated four hundred years. But I will punish the nation they serve as slaves, and afterward they will come out with great possessions." (NIV)

Genesis 41:25
Then Joseph said to Pharaoh, "The dreams of Pharaoh are one; God has shown Pharaoh what He is about to do." (NKJV)

Genesis 41:38
And Pharaoh said to his servants, "Can we find such a one as this, a man in whom is the Spirit of God?" (NKJV)

Exodus 7:3–5
"And I will harden Pharaoh's heart, and multiply My signs and My wonders in the land of Egypt. But Pharaoh will not heed you so that I may lay My hand on Egypt and bring My armies and My people, the children of Israel, out of the land of Egypt by great judgments.

And the Egyptians shall know that I am the Lord, when I stretch out My hand on Egypt and bring out the children of Israel from among them." (NKJV)

Exodus 9:12
But the Lord hardened the heart of Pharaoh; and he did not heed them, just as the Lord had spoken to Moses. (NKJV)

Exodus 10:20
But the Lord hardened Pharaoh's heart, and he did not let the children of Israel go. (NKJV)

Exodus 10:27
But the Lord hardened Pharaoh's heart, and he would not let them go. (NKJV)

Exodus 11:10
So Moses and Aaron did all these wonders before Pharaoh; and the Lord hardened Pharaoh's heart, and he did not let the Children of Israel go out of his land. (NKJV)

Exodus 12:40
Now the Length of time the Israelite people lived in Egypt was 430 years. (NIV)

Exodus 20:3–11
"You shall have no other gods before me. You shall not make for yourself an idol in the form of anything in heaven above or on the earth beneath or in the waters below You shall not bow down to them or worship them; for I, the Lord your God, am a jealous God, punishing the children for the sin of the fathers to the third and fourth generation of those who hate me, but showing love to a thousand generations of those who love me and keep my commandments. You shall not misuse the name of the Lord your

God, for the Lord will not hold anyone guiltless who misuses His name. Remember the Sabbath day by keeping it holy. Six days you shall labor and do all your work, but the seventh day is a Sabbath to the Lord your God. On it you shall not do any work, neither you, nor your son or daughter, nor our manservant or maidservant, nor your animals, nor the alien within your gates. For in six days the Lord made the heavens and the earth, the sea, and all that is in them, but He rested on the seventh day. Therefore the Lord blessed the Sabbath day and made it holy." (NIV)

Numbers 1:2–3
"Take a census of all the congregation of the children of Israel, by their families by their fathers' houses, according to the number of names, every male individually, from twenty years old and above-all who are able to go to war in Israel." (NKJV)

Numbers 11:25
Then the Lord came down in the cloud, and spoke to him, and took of the Spirit that was upon him, and placed the same upon the seventy elders; and it happened, when the Spirit rested upon them, that they prophesied, although they never did so again. (NKJV)

Numbers 27:18
And the Lord said to Moses: "Take Joshua the son of Nun with you, a man in whom is the Spirit and lay your hand on him." (NKJV)

Deuteronomy 28:1–14
If you fully obey the Lord your God and carefully follow all His commands I give you today, the Lord your God will set you high above all the nations on earth. All these blessings will come on you and accompany you if you obey the Lord your God: You will be blessed in the city and blessed in the country. The fruit of your womb will be blessed, and the crops of your land and the young of your livestock – the calves of your herds and the lams of your

flocks. Your basket and your kneading trough will be blessed. You will be blessed when you come in and blessed when you go out. The Lord will grant that the enemies who rise up against you will be defeated before you. They will come at you from one direction but flee from you in seven, the Lord will send a blessing on your barns and on everything you put your hand to. The Lord your God will bless you in the land He is giving you. The Lord will establish you as His holy people, as He promised you on oath, if you keep the commands of the Lord your God and walk in obedience to Him. Then all the peoples on earth will see that you are called by the name of the Lord, and they will fear you. The Lord will grant you abundant prosperity – in the fruit of your womb, the young of your livestock and the crops of your ground - in the land He swore to your ancestors to give you. The Lord will open the heavens, the storehouses of His bounty, to send rain on your land in season and to bless all the work of your hands. You will lend to many nations but will borrow from none. The Lord will make you the head, not the tail. If you pay attention to the commands of the Lord your God that I give you this day and carefully follow them you will always be at the top, never at the bottom. Do not turn aside from any of the commands I give you today to the right or to the left, following other gods and serving them. (NIV)

Deuteronomy 28:15–68
However, if you do not obey the Lord your God and do not carefully follow all His commands and decrees I am giving you today, all these curses will come on you and overtake you: You will be cursed in the city and cursed in the country. Your basket and your kneading trough will be cursed. The fruit of your womb will be cursed, and the crops of your land, and the calves of your herds and the lambs of your flocks. You will be cursed when you come in and cursed when you go out. The Lord will send on you curses, confusion and rebuke in everything you put your hand to, until you are destroyed and come to sudden ruin because of the evil you have done in

forsaking Him. The Lord will plague you with diseases until He has destroyed you from the land you are entering to possess. The Lord will strike you with wasting disease, with fever and inflammation, with scorching heat and drought, with blight and mildew, which will plague you until you perish. The sky over your head will be bronze, the ground beneath you iron. The Lord will turn the rain of your country into dust and powder; it will come down from the skies until you are destroyed. The Lord will cause you to be defeated before your enemies. You will come at them from one direction but flee from them in seven, and you will become a thing of horror to all the kingdoms on earth. Your carcasses will be food for all the birds and the wild animals, and there will be no one to frighten them away. The Lord will afflict you with the boils of Egypt and with tumors, festering sores and the itch, from which you cannot be cured. The Lord will afflict you with madness, blindness and confusion of mind. At midday you will grope about like a blind person in the dark. You will be unsuccessful in everything you do; day after day you will be oppressed and robbed, with no one to rescue you. You will be pledged to be married to a woman, but another will take her and rape her. You will build a house, but you will not live in it. You will plant a vineyard, but you will not even begin to enjoy its fruit. Your ox will be slaughtered before your eyes, but you will eat none of it. Your donkey will be forcibly taken from you and will not be returned. Your sheep will be given to your enemies, and no one will rescue them. Your sons and daughters will be given to another nation, and you will wear out your eyes watching for the day after day, powerless to lift a hand. A people that you do not know will eat what your land and labor produce, and you will have nothing but cruel oppression all your days. The sights you see will drive you mad. The Lord will afflict your knees and legs with painful boils that cannot be cured, spreading from the soles of your feet to the top of your head. The Lord will drive you and the king you set over you to a nation unknown to you or your ancestors. There you will worship other gods, gods of wood and stone. You will become a thing of horror, a byword and an object of ridicule among all the peoples where the Lord will drive you. You will sow much seed in the field but you will harvest little, because locusts will devour it. You will plant vineyards and cultivate them but you will not drink the wine or gather the grapes, because worms will eat them. You will have olive trees throughout your country but you will not use the oil, because the olives will drop off. You will have sons and daughters but you will not keep them, because they will go into captivity. Swarms of locusts will take over all your trees and the crops of your land. The foreigners who reside among you will rise above you higher and higher, but you will sink lower and lower. They will lend to you, but you will not lend to them. They will be the head, but you will be the tail. All these curses will come on you. They will pursue you and overtake you until you are destroyed, because you did not obey the Lord your God and observe the commands and decrees He gave you. They will be a sign and a wonder to you and your descendants forever. Because you did not serve the Lord your God joyfully and gladly in the time of prosperity, therefore in hunger and thirst, in nakedness and dire poverty, you will serve the enemies the Lord sends against you. He will put an iron yoke on your neck until He has destroyed you. The Lord will bring a nation against you from far away, from the ends of the earth, like an eagle swooping down, a nation whose language you will not understand, a fierce-looking nation without respect for the old or pity for the young. They will devour the young of your livestock and the crops of your land and the crops of your land until you are destroyed. They will leave you no grain, new wine or olive oil, nor any calves of your herds or lambs of your flocks until you are ruined. They will lay siege to all the cities throughout your land until the high fortified walls in which you trust fall down. They will besiege all the cities throughout the land the Lord your God is giving you. Because of the suffering your enemy will inflict on you during the siege, you will eat the fruit of the womb, the flesh of the sons and daughters the Lord your God has given you. Even the most gentle and sensitive man among you will have no compassion on his own brother or the wife he loves or his surviving children, and he will not give to one of them any of the flesh of his children that he is eating. It will be all he has left because of the suffering your enemy will inflict on you during the siege of all y our cities. The most gentle and sensitive woman among you – so sensitive and gentle that she would not venture to touch the ground with the sole of her foot – will begrudge the husband she loves and her own son or daughter the afterbirth from her womb and the children she bears. For in her dire need she intends to eat them secretly because of the suffering your enemy will inflict on you during the siege of your cities. If you do not carefully follow all the words of this law, which are written in this book, and do not revere this glorious and awesome name – the Lord your God – the Lord will send fearful plagues on you and your descendants, harsh and prolonged disasters, and severe and lingering illnesses. He will bring on you all the diseases of Egypt that you dreaded, and they will cling to you. The Lord will also bring on you every kind of sickness and disaster not recorded in this Book of the Law, until you are destroyed. You who were as numerous as the stars in the sky will be left but few in number, because you did not obey the Lord your God. Just as it pleased the Lord to make you prosper and increase in number, so it will please Him to ruin and destroy you. You will be uprooted from the land you are entering to possess. Then the Lord will scatter you among all nations, from one end of the earth to the other. There you will worship other gods – gods of wood and stone, which neither you nor your ancestors have known. Among those nations you will find no repose, no resting place for the sole of your foot. There the Lord will give you an anxious mind, eyes weary with longing, and a despairing heart. You will live in constant suspense, filled with dread both night and day, never sure of your life. In the morning you will say, "If only it were evening!" and in the evening, "If only it were morning!" – because of the terror that will fill your hearts and the sights that your eyes will see. The Lord will send you back in ships to Egypt on a journey I said you should never make again. There you will offer yourselves for sale to your enemies as male and female slaves, but no one will buy you. (NIV)

Deuteronomy 30:19–20
"I call heaven and earth as witnesses today against you, that I have set before you life and death, blessing and curing; therefore choose life, that both you and your descendants may live; that you may love the Lord your God, that you may obey His voice, and that you may cling to Him, for He is your life and the length of our days; and that you may dwell in the land which the Lord swore to your fathers, to Abraham, Isaac and Jacob, to give them." (NKJV)

Deuteronomy 33:27
The eternal God is your refuge, And underneath are the everlasting arms; (NKJV)

Joshua 24:2–14
Joshua said to all the people, "This is what the Lord the God of Israel says: 'Long ago your forefathers, including Terah the father of Abraham and Nahor, lived beyond the river and worshipped other gods. But I took your father Abraham from the land beyond the River and led him throughout Canaan and gave him many descendants. I gave him Isaac, and to Isaac I gave Jacob and Esau. I assigned the hill country of Seir to Esau, but Jacob and his sons went down to Egypt. Then I sent Moses and Aaron and I afflicted the Egyptians by what I did there, and I brought you out. When I brought your fathers out of Egypt you came to the sea and the Egyptians pursued them with chariots and horsemen as far as the Red Sea. But they cried to the Lord for help, and He put darkness between you and the Egyptians; He brought the sea over them and covered them. You saw with your own eyes what I did to the Egyptians. Then you lived in the desert for a long time. I brought you to the land of the Amorites who lived east of the Jordan. They fought against you, but I gave them into your hands. I destroyed

them from before you and you took possession of their land. When Balak son of Zippor, the king of Moab, prepared to fight against Israel, he sent for Balaam son of Beor to put a curse on you. But I would not listen to Balaam, so he blessed you again and again and I delivered you out of his hand. Then you crossed the Jordan and came to Jericho. The citizens of Jericho fought against you as did also the Amorites, Perizzites Canaanites Hittites Girgashites Hivites and Jebusites but I gave them into your hands. I sent the hornet ahead of you which drove them out before you – also the two Amorite kings. You did not do it with your own sword and bow. So I gave you a land on which you did not toil and cities you did not build, and you live in them and eat from vineyards and olive groves that you did not plant,'" (NIV)

Judges 3:10
The Spirit of the Lord came upon him, and he judged Israel. He went out to war, (NKJV)

1 Samuel 10:9–10
As Saul turned to leave Samuel, God changed Saul's heart, and all these signs were fulfilled that day. When they arrived at Gibeah a procession of prophets met him; the Spirit of God came upon him in power, and he joined in their prophesying. (NIV)

1 Samuel 13:14
"But now your kingdom will not endure; the Lord has sought out a man after His own heart and appointed him ruler of his people, because you have not kept the Lord's command." (NIV)

1 Samuel 16:13
Then Samuel took the horn of oil and anointed him in the midst of his brothers; and the Spirit of the Lord came upon David from that day forward. (NKJV)

1 Samuel 16:14–15
Now the Spirit of the Lord had departed from Saul, and an evil spirit from the Lord tormented him. Saul's attendants said to him, "See, an evil spirit from God is tormenting you." (NIV)

1 Samuel 18:10
The next day an evil spirit from God came forcefully upon Saul. (NIV)

1 Kings 22:19–23
Micaiah continued, "Therefore hear the word of the Lord: I saw the Lord sitting on His throne with all the host of heaven standing around Him on His right and on His left. And the Lord said, 'Who will entice Ahab into attacking Ramoth Gilead and going to his death there?' One suggested this and another that. Finally, a spirit came forward, stood before the Lord and said, 'I will entice him.' 'By what means?' the Lord asked. 'I will go out and be a lying spirit in the mouths of all his prophets,' he said. 'You will succeed in enticing him,' said the Lord. 'Go and do it.' So now the Lord has put a lying spirit in the mouths of all these prophets of yours. The Lord has decreed disaster for you." (NIV)

Job 1:12
And the Lord said to Satan, "Behold, all that he has is in your power; only do not lay a hand on his person." (NKJV)

Job 2:6
And the Lord said to Satan, "Behold, he is in your hand, but spare his life." (NKJV)

Job 12:10
In His hand is the life of every creature and the breath of all mankind. (NIV)

Job 33:4
The Spirit of God has made me, And the breath of the Almighty gives me life. (NKJV)

Job 34:13–15
Who appointed Him over the earth? Who put Him in charge of the whole world? If it were His intention and he withdrew His Spirit and breath, all humanity would perish together and mankind would return to the dust, (NIV)

Psalms 23:3–4
He restores my soul; He leads me in the paths of righteousness For His name's sake. Yea, though I walk through the valley of the shadow of death, I will fear no evil; For You are with me; Your rod and Your staff, they comfort me. (NKJV)

Psalms 90:4
For a thousand years in Your sight Are like yesterday when it is past, and like a watch in the night. (NKJV)

Ecclesiastes 9:5
For the living know that they will die; but the dead know nothing, and they have no more reward, for the memory of them is forgotten. Also their love, their hatred, and their envy have now perished; Nevermore will they have a share in anything done under the sun. (NKJV)

Ecclesiastes 9:11
I returned and saw under the sun that – the race is not to the swift, nor the battle to the strong nor bread to the wise, nor riches to men of understanding, nor favor to men of skill; but time and chance happen to them all. (NKJV)

Ecclesiastes 12:7
Then the dust will return to the earth as it was, and the spirit will return to God who gave it. (NKJV)

Ecclesiastes 12:12–14
...Of making many books there is no end, and much study wearies the body. Now all has been heard; here is the conclusion of the matter: Fear God and keep His commandments, for this is the whole duty of man. For God will bring every deed into judgment, including every hidden thing, whether it is good or evil. (NIV)

Isaiah 9:2
The people walking in darkness have seen a great light; on those living in the land of the shadow of death a light has dawned. (NIV)

Isaiah 14:12–15
How you are fallen from heaven, O Lucifer, son of the morning! How you are cut down to the ground, you who weakened the nations! For you have said in your heart: "I will ascend into heaven, I will exalt my throne above the stars of God; I will also sit on the mount of the congregation on the farthest sides of the north; I will ascend above the heights of the clouds I will be like the Most High." Yet you shall be brought down to Sheol, to the lowest depths of the Pit. (NKJV)

Isaiah 44:2
This is what the Lord says – He who made you, who formed you in the womb, and who will help you. Do not be afraid. (NIV)

Isaiah 44:24
Thus says the Lord, your Redeemer, And He who formed you from the womb: "I am the Lord, who makes all things, who stretches out the heavens all alone, who spreads abroad the earth by Myself;" (NKJV)

Isaiah 48:17
This is what the Lord says – your Redeemer, the Holy One of Israel: "I am the Lord your God, who teaches you what is best for you, who directs you in the way you should go." (NIV)

Isaiah 64:8
But now, O Lord, You are our Father; We are the clay, and You are the potter; And all we are the work of your hand. (NKJV)

Jeremiah 18:3–6
So I went down to the potter's house, and I saw him working at the wheel. But the pot he was shaping from the clay was marred in his hands; so the potter formed it into another pot, shaping it as seemed best to him. Then the word of the Lord came to me: "O house of Israel, can I not do with you as this potter does?" Declares the Lord. Like clay in the hand of the potter, so are you in my hand, O house of Israel." (NIV)

Jeremiah 31:31–34
"The time is coming," declares the Lord, "when I will make a new covenant with the house of Israel and with the house of Judah. It will not be like the covenant I made with their forefathers when I took them by the hand to lead them out of Egypt, because they broke my covenant, though I was a husband to them," declares the Lord. "This is the covenant I will make with the house of Israel after that time," declares the Lord. "I will put my law in their minds and write it on their hearts. I will be their God, and they will be my people. No longer will a man teach his neighbor, or a man his brother, saying, 'Know the Lord,' because they will all know me, from the least of them to the greatest," declares the Lord. "For I will forgive their wickedness and will remember their sins no more." (NIV)

Ezekiel 18:4
"Behold, all souls are Mine; The soul of the father as well as the soul of the son is Mine; The soul who sins shall die." (NKJV)

Micah 3:8
But truly I am full of power by the Spirit of the Lord, and of justice and might, to declare to Jacob his transgression and to Israel his sin. (NKJV)

Micah 6:8
He has shown you, O man, what is good; And what does the Lord require of you but to do justly, To love mercy, And to walk humbly with your God? (NKJV)

Zechariah 12:1
This is the word of the Lord concerning Israel. The Lord, who stretches out the heavens who lays the foundation of the earth, and who forms the spirit of man within him, declares: (NIV)

Matthew 3:13–17
Then Jesus came from Galilee to the Jordan to be baptized by John. But John tried to deter Him saying, "I need to be baptized by you, and do you come to me?" Jesus replied, "Let it be so now; it is proper for us to do this to fulfill all righteousness." Then John consented. As soon as Jesus was baptized, He went up out of the water. At that moment heaven was opened, and He saw the Spirit of God descending like a dove and lighting on Him. And lo a voice from heaven, saying, "This is my beloved Son, in whom I am well pleased." (NIV)

Matthew 4:1–10
Then Jesus was led by the Spirit into the wilderness to be tempted by the devil. After fasting forty days and forty nights, He was hungry. The tempter came to him and said, "If you are the Son of God, tell these stones to become bread." Jesus answered, "It is written: 'Man shall not live on bread alone, but on every word that comes from the mouth of God.'" Then the devil took him to the holy city and had him stand on the highest point of the temple. "If you are the Son of God," he said, "throw yourself down, for it is written: "'He

will command his angels concerning you, and they will lift you up in their hands, so that you will not strike your foot against a stone.'" Jesus answered him, "It is also written: 'Do not put the Lord your God to the test.'" Again, the devil took him to a very high mountain and showed him all the kingdoms of the world and their splendor. "All this I will give you," he said, "if you will bow down and worship me." Jesus said to him, "Away from me Satan! For it is written: 'Worship the Lord your God and serve him only.'" (NIV)

Matthew 5:3–12
"Blessed are the poor in spirit, for theirs is the kingdom of heaven. Blessed are those who mourn, for they shall be comforted. Blessed are the meek, for they shall inherit the earth. Blessed are those who hunger and thirst for righteousness, for they shall be filled. Blessed are the merciful, for they shall obtain mercy. Blessed are the pure in heart, for they shall see God. Blessed are the peacemakers, for they shall be called sons of God. Blessed are those who are persecuted for righteousness' sake, for theirs is the kingdom of heaven. Blessed are you when they revile and persecute you and say all kinds of evil against you falsely for My sake. Rejoice and be exceedingly glad, for great is your reward in heaven, for so they persecuted the prophets who were before you." (NKJV)

Matthew 5:17
"Do not think that I came to destroy the Law or the Prophets. I did not come to destroy but to fulfill." (NKJV)

Matthew 7:12
"So in everything, do to others what you would have them do to you, for this sums up the Law and the Prophets." (NIV)

Matthew 7:28–29
And so it was, when Jesus had ended these sayings, that the people were astonished at His teaching, for He taught them as one having authority, and not as the scribes. (NKJV)

Matthew 8:21–22
Then another of His disciples said to Him, "Lord, let me first go and bury my father." But Jesus said to him, "Follow Me, and let the dead bury their own dead." (NKJV)

Matthew 8:29
"What do you want with us Son of God?" they shouted. "Have you come here to torture us before the appointed time?" (NIV)

Matthew 10:28
"Do not be afraid of those who kill the body but cannot kill the soul. Rather, be afraid of the One who can destroy both soul and body in hell." (NIV)

Matthew 11:25–27
At that time Jesus answered and said, "I thank You, Father, Lord of heaven and earth, that You have hidden these things from the wise and prudent and have revealed them to babes. Even so, Father, for so it seemed good in Your sight. All things have been delivered to Me by My Father, and no one knows the Son except the Father. Nor does anyone know the Father except the Son, and the one to whom the Son wills to reveal Him. Come to Me all you who labor and are heavy laden, and I will give you rest. Take My yoke upon you and learn from Me, for I am gentle and lowly in heart, and you will find rest for your souls. For My yoke is easy and My burden is light." (NKJV)

Matthew 12:18
"Behold! My Servant whom I have chosen, My Beloved in whom My soul is well pleased! I will put My Spirit upon Him, and He will declare justice to the Gentiles." (NKJV)

Matthew 13:10–15
The disciples came to Him and asked, "Why do you speak to the people in parables?" He replied, "Because the knowledge of the secrets

of the kingdom of heaven has been given to you, but not to them. Whoever has will be given more, and they will have an abundance. Whoever does not have, even what they have will be taken from them. This is why I speak to them in parables: Though seeing they do not see, though hearing, they do not hear or understand. In them is fulfilled the prophecy of Isaiah: 'You will be ever hearing but never understanding; you will be ever seeing but never perceiving. For this people's heart has become calloused; they hardly hear with their ears, and they have closed their eyes. Otherwise they might see with their eyes, hear with their ears, understand with their hearts and turn, and I would heal them.'" (NIV)

Matthew 15:15–16
Then Peter answered and said to Him, "Explain this parable to us." So Jesus said, "Are you also still without understanding?" (NKJV)

Matthew 16:8–9
But Jesus, being aware of it, said to them, "O you of little faith, why do you reason among yourselves because you have brought no bread? Do you not yet understand, or remember the five loaves of the five thousand and how many baskets you took up?" (NKJV)

Matthew 19:4–5
"Haven't you read," he replied, "that at the beginning the Creator 'made them male and female,' and said, 'For this reason a man will leave his father and mother and be united to his wife, and they will become one flesh'? (NIV)

Matthew 19:26
But Jesus looked at them and said to them, "With men this is impossible, but with God all things are possible." (NKJV)

Matthew 22:14
"For many are called, but few are chosen." (NKJV)

Matthew 22:31–33
But concerning the resurrection of the dead, have you not read what was spoken to you by God, saying, "I am the God of Abraham, the God of Isaac, and the God of Jacob? God is not the God of the dead, but of the living." (NKJV)

Matthew 22:37–40
Jesus said to him, "You shall love the Lord your God with all your heart, with all your soul, and with all your mind. This is the first and great commandment. And the second is like it: You shall love your neighbor as yourself. On these two commandments hang all the Law and the Prophets." (NKJV)

Matthew 24:36
"No one knows about that day or hour, not even the angels in heaven nor the Son but only the Father." (NIV)

Matthew 26:18
He replied, "Go into the city to a certain man and tell him, 'The Teacher says; My appointed time is near. I am going to celebrate the Passover with my disciples at your house.'" (NIV)

Matthew 26:53
"Or do you think that I cannot now pray to My Father, and He will provide Me with more than twelve legions of angels?" (NKJV)

Matthew 27:46
And about the ninth hour Jesus cried out with a loud voice, saying, "Eli, Eli, lama sabachthani?" that is, "My God, My God, why have you forsaken Me?" (NKJV)

Mark 1:14
Now after John was put in prison, Jesus came to Galilee, preaching the gospel of the kingdom of God, and saying, "The time is fulfilled,

and the kingdom of God is at hand. Repent, and believe in the gospel." (NKJV)

Mark 4:10–13
When He was alone, the Twelve and the others around Him asked Him about the parables. He told them, "The secret of the kingdom of God has been given to you. But to those on the outside everything is said in parables so that, 'they may be ever seeing but never perceiving, and ever hearing but never understanding; otherwise they might turn and be forgiven!' then Jesus said to them, 'Don't you understand this parable? How then will you understand any parable?'" (NIV)

Mark 8:21
He said to them, "Do you still not understand?" (NIV)

Mark 9:32
But they did not understand this saying, and were afraid to ask Him. (NKJV)

Mark 13:32
"But of that day and hour no one knows, not even the angels in heaven, nor the Son, but only the Father." (NKJV)

Luke 1:79
"to give light to those who sit in darkness and the shadow of death, To guide our feet into the way of peace." (NKJV)

Luke 9:45
But they did not understand this saying, and it was hidden from them so that they did not perceive it; and they were afraid to ask Him about this saying. (NKJV)

Luke 10:18
And He said to them, "I saw Satan fall like lightning from heaven." (NKJV)

Luke 10:30–37
In reply Jesus said: "A man was going down from Jerusalem to Jericho, when he fell into the hands of robbers. They stripped him of his clothes, beat him and went away, leaving him half dead. A priest happened to be going down the same road, and when he saw the man, he passed by on the other side. So too, a Levite, when he came to the place and saw him, passed by on the other side. But a Samaritan, as he traveled, came where the man was; and when he saw him, he took pity on him. He went to him and bandaged his wounds, pouring on oil and wine. Then he put the man on his own donkey, took him to an inn and took care of him. The next day he took out two silver coins and gave them to the innkeeper. Look after him, he said, and when I return, I will reimburse you for any extra expense you may have. Which of these three do you think was a neighbor to the man who fell into the hands of robbers?" The expert in the law replied, "The one who had mercy on him." Jesus told him, "Go and do likewise." (NIV)

Luke 21:24
"And they will fall by the edge of the sword, and be led away captive into all nations. And Jerusalem will be trampled by the Gentiles until the times of the Gentiles are fulfilled." (NKJV)

Luke 23:46
And when Jesus had cried out with a loud voice, He said, "Father, into Your hands I commit My spirit." Having said this, He breathed His last. (NKJV)

Luke 24:44–47
Then He said to them, "These are the words which I spoke to you while I was still with you, that all things must be fulfilled which

were written in the Law of Moses and the Prophets and the Psalms concerning Me." And He opened their understanding, that they might comprehend the Scriptures. Then He said to them, "Thus it is written and thus it was necessary for the Christ to suffer and to rise from the dead the third day, and that repentance and remission of sins should be preached in His name to all nations, beginning at Jerusalem." (NKJV)

John 1:1
In the beginning was the Word, and the Word was with God, and the Word was God. (NKJV)

John 1:12–14
Yet to all who received Him, to those who believed in His name, He gave the right to become children of God – children born not of natural descent, nor of human decision or a husband's will, but born of God. The Word became flesh and made His dwelling among us. We have seen His glory, the glory of the one and only Son, who came from the Father, full of grace and truth. (NIV)

John 3:13
"No one has ascended to heaven but He who came down from heaven, that is, the Son of Man who is in heaven." (NKJV)

John 3:16
For God so loved the world that He gave His one and only Son that whoever believes in Him shall not perish but have eternal life. (NKJV)

John 4:23–24
"But the hour is coming, and now is, when the true worshipers will worship the Father in Spirit and truth; for the Father is seeking such to worship Him. God is spirit, and those who worship Him must worship in Spirit and truth." (NKJV)

John 5:17
But Jesus answered them, "My Father has been working until now, and I have been working." (NKJV)

John 5:26–27
"For as the Father has life in Himself, so He has granted the Son to have life in Himself, and has given Him authority to judge also, because He is the Son of Man." (NKJV)

John 8:16–18
"And yet if I do judge, My judgment is true; for I am not alone, but I am with the Father who sent Me. It is also written in your law that the testimony of two men is true. I am One who bears witness of Myself, and the Father who sent Me bears witness of Me." (NKJV)

John 8:43–45
"Why is my language not clear to you? Because you are unable to hear what I say. You belong to your father, the devil, and you want to carry out your father's desire. He was a murderer from the beginning, not holding to the truth, for there is no truth in him. When he lies, he speaks his native language, for he is a liar and the father of lies." (NIV)

John 10:7–10
Then Jesus said to them again, "Most assuredly, I say to you, I am the door of the sheep. All who ever came before Me are thieves and robbers, but the sheep did not hear them. I am the door. If anyone enters by Me, he will be saved, and will go in and out and find pasture. The thief does not come except to steal, and to kill, and to destroy. I have come that they may have life, and that they may have it more abundantly." (NKJV)

John 10:30
"I and My Father are one." (NKJV)

John 10:34–38
Jesus answered them, "Is it not written in your law, 'I said, "you are gods"'? If He called them 'gods', to whom the word of God came (and the Scripture cannot be broken), do you say of Him whom the Father sanctified and sent into the world, 'You are blaspheming,' because I said, 'I am the Son of God'? If I do not do the works of My Father, do not believe Me; but if I do, though you do not believe Me, believe the works, that you may know and believe that the Father is in Me, and I in Him." (NKJV)

John 13:34–35
"A new commandment I give to you, that you love one another; as I have loved you, that you also love one another. By this all will know that you are My disciples, if you have love for one another." (NKJV)

John 14:2–4
"In My Father's house are many mansions; if it were not so, I would have told you. I go to prepare a place for you. And if I go and prepare a place for you, I will come again and receive you to Myself; that where I am, there you may be also. And where I go you know, and the way you know." (NKJV)

John 14:6
Jesus said to him, "I am the way, the truth, and the life. No one comes to the Father except through Me." (NKJV)

John 14:9–11
Jesus said to him, "Have I been with you so long, and yet you have not known Me, Philip? He who has seen Me has seen the Father; so how can you say, 'Show us the Father'? Do you not believe that I am in the Father, and the Father in Me? The words that I speak to you I do not speak on My own authority; but the Father who dwells in Me does the works. Believe me that I am in the Father and the Father in Me, or else believe Me for the sake of the works themselves." (NKJV)

John 14:15–17
"If you love Me, keep My commandments. And I will pray the Father, and He will give you another Helper, that He may abide with you forever - the Spirit of truth, whom the world cannot receive, because it neither sees Him nor knows Him, for He dwells with you and will be in you." (NKJV)

John 14:23
Jesus answered and said to him, "If anyone loves Me, he will keep My word; and My Father will love him, and We will come to him and make Our home with him." (NKJV)

John 14:25–27
"All this I have spoken while still with you. But the Counselor, the Holy Spirit, whom the Father will send in my name, will teach you all things and will remind you of everything I have said to you. Peace I leave with you; my peace I give you. I do not give to you as the world gives. Do not let your hearts be troubled and do not be afraid." (NIV)

John 15:26
"When the Counselor comes, whom I will send to you from the Father, the Spirit of truth who goes out from the Father, he will testify about me. And you also must testify, for you have been with me from the beginning." (NIV)

John 16:7
"Nevertheless I tell you the truth. It is to your advantage that I go away; for if I do not go away, the Helper will not come to you; but if I depart, I will send Him to you." (NKJV)

John 16:13
"But when he, the Spirit of truth, comes, he will guide you into all truth. He will not speak on his own; he will speak only what he hears…" (NKJV)

John 16:23
"And in that day you will ask Me nothing. Most assuredly, I say to you, whatever you ask the Father in My name He will give you." (NIV)

John 18:36
Jesus answered, "My kingdom is not of this world. If My kingdom were of this world, My servants would fight, so that I should not be delivered to the Jews; but now My kingdom is not from here." (NKJV)

John 17:20–23
I do not pray for these alone, but also for those who will believe in Me through their word; that they all may be one, as You, Father, are in Me, and I in You; that they also may be one in Us, that the world may believe that You sent Me. And the glory which You gave Me I have given them, that they may be one just as We are one: I in them, and You in Me; that they may be made perfect in one and that the world may know that You have sent Me, and have loved them as You have loved Me. (NKJV)

John 20:17
Jesus said to her, "Do not cling to Me, for I have not yet ascended to My Father; but go to My brethren and say to them, 'I am ascending to My Father and your Father, and to My God and your God.'" (NKJV)

Acts 2:1–4
When the day of Pentecost came, they were all together in one place. Suddenly a sound like the blowing of a violent wind came from heaven and filled the whole house where they were sitting. They saw what seemed to be tongues of fire that separated and came to rest on each of them. All of them were filled with the Holy Spirit… (NIV)

Acts 2:16–18
No, this is what was spoken by the prophet Joel: "In the last days, God says, I will pour out my Spirit on all people. Your sons and daughters will prophesy, your young men will see visions your old men will dream dreams. Even on my servants, both men and women I will pour out my Spirit in those days and they will prophesy." (NIV)

Acts 2:34
For David did not ascend to heaven, and yet he said, The Lord said to my Lord: "Sit at my right hand." (NIV)

Acts 2:37–39
When the people heard this, they were cut to the heart and said to Peter and the other apostles, Brothers, what shall we do? Peter replied, Repent and be baptized, every one of you, in the name of Jesus Christ for the forgiveness of your sins. And you will receive the gift of the Holy Spirit. The promise is for you and your children and for all who are far off – for all whom the Lord our God will call. (NIV)

Acts 8:38–39
And he gave orders to stop the chariot. Then both Philip and the eunuch went down into the water and Philip baptized him. When they came up out of the water, the Spirit of the Lord suddenly took Philip away and the eunuch did not see him again, but went on his way rejoicing. (NIV)

Acts 10:45
The circumcised believers who had come with Peter were astonished that the gift of the Holy Spirit had been poured out even on the Gentiles. (NIV)

Acts 13:22
After removing Saul, He made David their king. He testified concerning him: "I have found David son of Jesse, a man after my own heart; he will do everything I want him to do." (NIV)

Acts 15:24
Since we have heard that some who went out from us have troubled you with words, unsettling your souls, saying, "You must be circumcised and keep the law - to whom we gave no such commandment –" (NKJV)

Acts 17:24–27
The God who made the world and everything in it is the Lord of heaven and earth and does not live in temples built by hands. And He is not served by human hands, as if He needed anything, because He Himself gives all men life and breath and everything else. From one man He made every nation of men, that they should inhabit the whole earth; and He determined the times set for them and the exact places where they should live. God did this so that men would seek Him and perhaps reach out for Him and find Him, though He is not far from each one of us. (NIV)

Romans 2:4
Or do you show contempt for the riches of His kindness, forbearance and patience, not realizing that God's kindness is intended to lead you to repentance? (NIV)

Romans 3:23
...For all have sinned and fall short of the glory of God, (NIV)

Romans 5:2–4
And we boast in the hope of the glory of God. Not only so, but we also glory in our sufferings, because we know that suffering produces perseverance; perseverance, character; and character, hope. (NIV)

Romans 6:11
Likewise you also, reckon yourselves to be dead indeed to sin, but alive to God in Christ Jesus our Lord. (NKJV)

Romans 6:23
For the wages of sin is death, but the gift of God is eternal life in Christ Jesus our Lord. (NIV)

Romans 7:4–6
Therefore, my brethren, you also have become dead to the law through the body of Christ, that you may be married to another – to Him who was raised from the dead, that we should bear fruit to God. For when we were in the flesh, the sinful passions which were aroused by the law were at work in our members to bear fruit to death. But now we have been delivered from the law, having died to what we were held by, so that we should serve in the newness of the Spirit and not in the oldness of the letter. (NKJV)

Romans 8:1–2
There is therefore now no condemnation to those who are in Christ Jesus, who do not walk according to the flesh, but according to the Spirit. For the law of the Spirit of life in Christ Jesus has made me free from the law of sin and death. (NKJV)

Romans 8:6–11
For to be carnally minded is death, but to be spiritually minded is life and peace. Because the carnal mind is enmity against God; for it is not subject to the law of God, nor indeed can be. So then, those who are in the flesh cannot please God. But you are not in the flesh but in the Spirit, if indeed the Spirit of God dwells in you. Now if anyone does not have the Spirit of Christ, he is not His. And if Christ is in you, the body is dead because of sin, but the Spirit is life because of righteousness. But if the Spirit of Him who raised Jesus from the dead dwells in you, He who raised Christ from the dead will also give life to your mortal bodies through His Spirit who dwells in you. (NKJV)

Romans 8:12–17
Therefore, brethren, we are debtors - not to the flesh, to live according to the flesh. For if you live according to the flesh you will die; but if by the Spirit you put to death the deeds of the body, you will live. For as many as are led by the Spirit of God, these are sons of God. For you did not receive the spirit of bondage again to fear, but you received the Spirit of adoption by whom we cry out, "Abba, Father". The Spirit Himself bears witness with our spirit that we are children of God, and if children, then heirs - heirs of God and joint heirs with Christ, if indeed we suffer with Him, that we may also be glorified together. (NKJV)

Romans 8:18–21
I consider that our present sufferings are not worth comparing with the glory that will be revealed in us. The creation waits in eager expectation for the sons of God to be revealed. For the creation was subject to frustration not by its own choice, but by the will of the one who subjected it, in hope that the creation itself will be liberated from its bondage to decay and brought into the glorious freedom of the children of God. (NIV)

Romans 8:28
And we know that in all things God works for the good of those who love Him, who have been called according to His purpose. (NIV)

Romans 8:39
neither height or depth, nor anything else in all creation, will be able to separate us from the love of God that is in Christ Jesus our Lord. (NIV)

Romans 9:9
For this was how the promise was stated: "At the appointed time I will return, and Sarah will have a son." (NIV)

Romans 9:11
(For the children not yet being born, nor having done any good or evil, that the purpose of God according to election might stand, not of works, but of Him who calls), (NKJV)

Romans 9:17–18
For Scripture says to Pharaoh: I raised you up for this very purpose, that I might display my power in you and that my name might be proclaimed in all the earth. Therefore God has mercy on whom He wants to have mercy, and He hardens whom He wants to harden. (NIV)

Romans 9:20–23
But who are you, O man, to talk back to God? Shall what is formed say to him who formed it, "Why did you make me like this?" Does not the potter have the right to make out of the same lump of clay some pottery for noble purposes and some for common use? What if God, choosing to show His wrath and make His power known, bore with great patience the objects of His wrath – prepared for destruction? What if He did this to make the riches of His glory known to the objects of His mercy, whom He prepared in advance for glory – even us, whom He also called... (NIV)

Romans 11:36
For of Him and through Him and to Him are all things, to whom be glory forever. Amen. (NKJV)

Romans 12
Therefore, I urge you brothers in view of God's mercy to offer your bodies as living sacrifices, holy and pleasing to God – this is your spiritual act of worship. Do not conform any longer to the pattern of this world, but be transformed by the renewing of your mind. Then you will be able to test and approve what God's will is – His good, pleasing and perfect will. For by the grace given me I say to every

one of you: Do not think of yourself more highly than you ought, but rather think of yourself with sober judgment, in accordance with the measure of faith God has given you. Just as each of us has one body with many members, and these members do not all have the same function, so in Christ we who are many from one body, and each member belongs to all the others. We have different gifts, according to the grace given us. If a man's gift is prophesying, let him use it in proportion to his faith. If it is serving, let him serve; if it is teaching, let him teach; if it is encouraging, let him encourage; if it is contributing to the needs of others, let him give generously; if it is leadership, let him govern diligently; if it is showing mercy, let him do it cheerfully. Love must be sincere. Hate what is evil; cling to what is good. Be devoted to one another in brotherly love. Honor one another above yourselves. Never be lacking in zeal, but keep your spiritual fervor, serving the Lord. Be joyful in hope, patient in affliction, faithful in prayer. Share with God's people who are in need. Practice hospitality. Bless those who persecute you; bless and do not curse. Rejoice with those who rejoice; mourn with those who mourn. Live in harmony with one another. Do not be proud, but be willing to associate with people of low position. Do not be conceited. Do not repay anyone evil for evil. Be careful to do what is right in the eyes of everybody. If it is possible, as far as it depends on you, live at peace with everyone. Do not take revenge, my friends, but leave room for God's wrath, for it is written: "It is mine to avenge; I will repay," says the Lord. On the contrary: "if your enemy is hungry, feed him; if he is thirsty, give him something to drink. In doing this, you will heap burning coals on his head." Do not be overcome by evil, but overcome evil with good. (NIV)

Romans 12:2
And do not be conformed to this world, but be transformed by the renewing of your mind that you may prove what is that good and acceptable and perfect will of God. (NKJV)

Romans 12:9–21
Love must be sincere. Hate what is evil; cling to what is good. Be devoted to one another in brotherly love. Honor one another above yourselves. Never be lacking in zeal, but keep your spiritual fervor, serving the Lord. Be joyful in hope, patient in affliction, faithful in prayer. Share with God's people who are in need. Practice hospitality. Bless those who persecute you; bless and do not curse. Rejoice with those who rejoice; mourn with those who mourn. Live in harmony with one another. Do not be proud, but be willing to associate with people of low position. Do not be conceited. Do not repay anyone evil for evil. Be careful to do what is right in the eyes of everybody. If it is possible, as far as it depends on you, live at peace with everyone. Do not take revenge, my friends, but leave room for God's wrath, for it is written: "It is mine to avenge; I will repay," says the Lord. On the contrary: "If your enemy is hungry feed him; if he is thirsty, give him something to drink. In doing this, you will heap burning coals on his head. Do not be overcome by evil, but overcome evil with good." (NIV)

Romans 13:8–10
Let no debt remain outstanding, except the continuing debt to love one another, for whoever loves others has fulfilled the law. The commandments, You shall not commit adultery, You shall not murder, You shall not steal, You shall not covet, and whatever other command there may be, are summed up in this one command: Love your neighbor as yourself. Love does no harm to a neighbor. Therefore love is the fulfillment of the law. (NIV)

Romans 14:9
For this very reason, Christ died and returned to life so that He might be Lord of both the dead and the living. (NIV)

1 Corinthians 2:6-8
However, we speak wisdom among those who are mature, yet not the wisdom of this age, nor of the rulers of this age, who are coming to

nothing. But we speak the wisdom of God in a mystery, the hidden wisdom which God ordained before the ages for our glory, which none of the rulers of this age knew, for had they known, they would not have crucified the Lord of Glory. (NKJV)

1 Corinthians 2:11–16
For what man knows the things of a man except the spirit of the man which is in him? Even so no one knows the things of God except the Spirit of God. Now we have received, not the spirit of the world, but the Spirit who is from God, that we might know the things that have been freely given to us by God. These things we also speak, not in words which man's wisdom teaches but which the Holy Spirit teaches, comparing spiritual things with spiritual. But the natural man does not receive the things of the Spirit of God, for they are foolishness to him; nor can he know them, because they are spiritually discerned. But he who is spiritual judges all things, yet he himself is rightly judged by no one. For who has known the mind of the Lord that he may instruct Him? But we have the mind of Christ. (NKJV)

1 Corinthians 4:5
Therefore judge nothing before the appointed time; wait until the Lord comes. (NIV)

1 Corinthians 6:17
But he who is joined to the Lord is one spirit with Him. (NKJV)

1 Corinthians 10:13
No temptation has seized you except what is common to man. And God is faithful; He will not let you be tempted beyond what you can bear. But when you are tempted, He will also provide a way out so that you can stand up under it. (NIV)

1 Corinthians 12:28–31
And in the church God has appointed first of all apostles, second prophets, third teachers, then workers of miracles, also those having gifts of healing, those able to help others, those with gifts of administration, and those speaking in different kinds of tongues. Are all apostles? Are all prophets? Are all teachers? Do all work miracles? Do all have gifts of healing? Do all interpret? But eagerly desire the greater gifts. (NIV)

1 Corinthians 13:1–8
Though I speak with the tongues of men and of angels, but have not love, I have become sounding brass or a clanging cymbal. And though I have the gift of prophecy, and understand all mysteries and all knowledge, and though I have all faith, so that I could move mountains, but have not love, I am nothing. And though I bestow all my goods to feed the poor, and though I give my body to be burned, but have not love, it profits me nothing. Love suffers long and is kind; love does not envy; love does not parade itself, is not puffed up; does not behave rudely, does not seek its own, is not provoked, thinks no evil; does not rejoice in iniquity, but rejoices in the truth; bears all things, believes all things. Hopes all things, endures all things. Love never fails. (NKJV)

1 Corinthians 15:24–28
Then the end will come, when He hands over the kingdom to God the Father after He has destroyed all dominion, authority and power. For He must reign until He has put all His enemies under His feet. The last enemy to be destroyed is death. For He "has put everything under His feet." Now when it says that "everything" has been put under Him, it is clear that this does not include God Himself, who put everything under Christ. When He has done this, then the Son Himself will be made subject to Him who put everything under Him, so that God may be all in all. (NIV)

1 Corinthians 15:45
And so it is written, "The first man Adam became a living being. The last Adam became a life-giving spirit." (NKJV)

1 Corinthians 15:50–56
Now this I say, brethren, that flesh and blood cannot inherit the kingdom of God; nor does corruption inherit incorruption. Behold, I tell you a mystery: We shall not all sleep, but we shall all be changed - in a moment, in the twinkling of an eye, at the last trumpet. For the trumpet will sound, and the dead will be raised incorruptible, and we shall be changed. For this corruptible must put on incorruption, and this mortal must put on immortality. For when this mortal has put on immortality, then shall be brought to pass the saying that is written: "Death is swallowed up in victory." "O Death, where is your sting? O Hades, where is your victory?" The sting of death is sin, and the strength of sin is the law. (NKJV)

2 Corinthians 3:4–6
And we have such trust through Christ toward God. Not that we are sufficient of ourselves to think of anything as being from ourselves, but our sufficiency is from God, who also made us sufficient as ministers of the New Covenant, not of the letter but of the Spirit; for the letter kills, but the Spirit gives life. (NKJV)

2 Corinthians 3:17
Now the Lord is the Spirit; and where the Spirit of the Lord is, there is liberty. (NKJV)

2 Corinthians 5:5
Now He who has prepared us for this very thing is God, who also has given us the Spirit as a guarantee. (NKJV)

2 Corinthians 5:17–19
Therefore, if anyone is in Christ, he is a new creation; old things have passed away; behold, all things have become new. Now all things are of God, who has reconciled us to Himself through Jesus Christ and has given us the ministry of reconciliation, that is that God was in Christ reconciling the world to Himself, not imputing their trespasses to them, and has committed to us the word of reconciliation. (NKJV)

2 Corinthians 6:16
…For you are the temple of the living God. As God has said: "I will dwell in them and walk among them. I will be their God, and they shall be my people." (NKJV)

2 Corinthians 6:18
"I will be a Father to you, and you will be my sons and daughters, says the Lord Almighty." (NKJV)

2 Corinthians 7:10
Godly sorrow brings repentance that leads to salvation and leaves no regret… (NIV)

Galatians 2:16–21
"knowing that a man is not justified by the works of the law but by faith in Jesus Christ, even we have believed in Christ Jesus, that we might be justified by faith in Christ and not by the works of the law; for by the works of the law no flesh shall be justified. But if, while we seek to be justified by Christ, we ourselves also are found sinners, is Christ therefore a minister of Sin? Certainly not! For if I build again those things which I destroyed, I make myself a transgressor. For I through the law died to the law that I might live to God. I have been crucified with Christ; it is no longer I who live, but Christ lives in me; and the life which I now live in the flesh I live by faith in the Son of God, who loved me and gave Himself for me. I do not set

aside the grace of God; for if righteousness comes through the law, then Christ died in vain." (NKJV)

Galatians 3:19–25
What purpose then does the law serve? It was added because of transgressions, till the Seed should come to whom the promise was made; and it was appointed through angels by the hand of a mediator. Now a mediator does not mediate for one only, but God is one. Is the law then against the promises of God? Certainly not! For if there had been a law given which could have given life truly righteousness would have been by the law. But the Scripture has confined all under sin, that the promise by faith in Jesus Christ might be given to those who believe. But before faith came, we were kept under guard by the law, kept for the faith which would afterward be revealed. Therefore the law was our tutor to bring us to Christ, that we might be justified by faith. But after faith has come, we are no longer under a tutor. (NKJV)

Galatians 3:26
For you are all sons of God through faith in Christ Jesus. For as many of you as were baptized into Christ have put on Christ. (NKJV)

Galatians 4:4–5
But when the fullness of the time had come, God sent forth His son, born of a woman, born under the law, to redeem those who were under the law, that we might receive the adoption as sons. (NKJV)

Galatians 5:6
...The only thing that counts is faith expressing itself through love. (NIV)

Galatians 5:14
For all the law is fulfilled in one word, even in this: "You shall love your neighbor as yourself." (NKJV)

Galatians 5:16–24
So I say, live by the Sprit and you will not gratify the desires of the sinful nature. For the sinful nature desires what is contrary to the Spirit, and the Spirit what is contrary to the sinful nature. They are in conflict with each other, so that you do not do what you want. But if you are led by the Spirit, you are not under law. The acts of the sinful nature are obvious: sexual immorality, impurity and debauchery; idolatry and witchcraft; hatred discord, jealousy, fits of rage, selfish ambition, dissensions, actions and envy; drunkenness, orgies, and the like. I warn you, as I did before, that those who live like this will not inherit the kingdom of God. But the fruit of the Spirit is love, joy, peace, patience, kindness, goodness, faithfulness, gentleness and self-control. Against such things there is no law. Those who belong to Christ Jesus have crucified the sinful nature with its passions and desires. Since we live by the Spirit, let us keep in step with the Spirit. Let us not become conceited, provoking and envying each other. (NIV)

Ephesians 1:4–12
just as He chose us in Him before the foundation of the world, that we should be holy and without blame before Him in love, having predestined us to adoption as sons by Jesus Christ to Himself, according to the good pleasure of His will, to the praise of the glory of His grace, by which He made us accepted in the Beloved. In Him we have redemption through His blood, the forgiveness of sins according to the riches of His grace which He made to abound toward us in all wisdom and prudence having made known to us the mystery of His will, according to His good pleasure which He purposed in Himself, that in the dispensation of the fullness of the times He might gather together in one all things in Christ, both which are in heaven and which are on hearth – in Him. In Him also we have obtained an inheritance, being predestined according to the purpose of Him who works all things according to the counsel of His will, that we who first trusted in Christ should be to the praise of His glory. (NKJV)

Ephesians 1:9–14
And He made known to us the mystery of His will according to His good pleasure, which He purposed in Christ, to be put into effect when the times will have reached their fulfillment – to bring all things in heaven and on earth together under one head, even Christ. In Him we were also chosen, having been predestined according to the plan of Him who works out everything in conformity with the purpose of His will, in order that we, who were the first to hope in Christ, might be for the praise of His glory. And you also were included in Christ when you heard the word of truth, the gospel of your salvation. Having believe you were marked in Him with a seal, the promised Holy Spirit, who is a deposit guaranteeing our inheritance until the redemption of those who are God's possession – to the praise of His glory. (NIV)

Ephesians 2:2
In which you once walked according to the course of this world, according to the prince of the power of the air, the spirit who now works in the sons of disobedience, (NKJV)

Ephesians 2:8–10
For by grace you have been saved through faith, and that not of yourselves; it is the gift of God, not of works, lest anyone should boast. For we are His workmanship, created in Christ Jesus for good works, which God prepared beforehand that we should walk in them. (NKJV)

Ephesians 3:3–6
how that by revelation He made known to me the mystery (as I have briefly written already, by which, when you read, you may understand my knowledge in the mystery of Christ), which in other ages was not made known to the sons of men, as it has now been revealed by the Spirit to His holy apostles and prophets; that the Gentiles should be fellow heirs, of the same body, and partakers of His promise in Christ through the gospel, (NKJV)

Ephesians 3:9–11
and to make all see what is the fellowship of the mystery, which from the beginning of the ages has been hidden in God who created all things through Jesus Christ; to the intent that now the manifold wisdom of God might be made known by the church to the principalities and powers in the heavenly places, according to the eternal purpose which He accomplished in Christ Jesus our Lord. (NKJV)

Ephesians 3:14–19
For this reason I kneel before the Father, from whom His whole family in heaven and on earth derives its name. I pray that out of His glorious riches He may strengthen you with power through His Spirit in your inner being, so that Christ may dwell in your hearts through faith. And I pray that you, being rooted and established in love, may have power, together with all the saints to grasp how wide and long and high and deep is the love of Christ, and to know this love that surpasses knowledge – that you may be filled to the measure of all the fullness or God. (NIV)

Ephesians 4:1–3
I, therefore, the prisoner of the Lord, beseech you to walk worthy of the calling with which you were called, with all lowliness and gentleness, with longsuffering, bearing with one another in love, endeavoring to keep the unity of the Spirit in the bond of peace. (NKJV)

Ephesians 4:7
But to each one of us grace was given according to the measure of Christ's gift. (NKJV)

Ephesians 4:12–13
For the equipping of the saints for the work of ministry, for the edifying of the body of Christ, till we all come to the unity of the

faith and of the knowledge of the Son of God, to a perfect man, to the measure of the stature of the fullness of Christ; (NKJV)

Ephesians 4:22–25
You were taught, with regard to your former way of life, to put off your old self, which is being corrupted by its deceitful desires; to be made new in the attitude of your minds; and to put on the new self, created to be like God in true righteousness and holiness. Therefore each of you must put off falsehood and speak truthfully to his neighbor, for we are all members of one body. (NIV)

Ephesians 4:29–32
Do not let any unwholesome talk come out of your mouths, but only what is helpful for building others up according to their needs, that it may benefit those who listen. And do not grieve the Holy Spirit of God, by whom you were sealed for the day of redemption. Get rid of all bitterness, rage and anger, brawling and slander, along with every form of malice. Be kind and compassionate to one another, forgiving each other, just as in Christ God forgave you. (NIV)

Ephesians 5:1–2
Therefore be imitators of God as dear children. And walk in love, as Christ also has loved us and given Himself for us, an offering and a sacrifice to God for a sweet-smelling aroma. (NKJV)

Philippians 2:12–13
Therefore, my beloved, as you have always obeyed, not as in my presence only, but now much more in my absence, work out your own salvation with fear and trembling; for it is God who works in you both to will and to do for His good pleasure. (NKJV)

Philippians 4:8–9
Finally, brethren, whatever things are true, whatever things are noble, whatever things are just, whatever things are pure, whatever

things are lovely, whatever things are of good report, if there is any virtue and if there is anything praiseworthy--meditate on these things. The things which you learned and received and heard and saw in me, these do, and the God of peace will be with you. (NKJV)

Colossians 1:16–17
For by Him all things were created that are in heaven and that are on earth, visible and invisible, whether thrones or dominions or principalities or powers. All things were created through Him and for Him. (NKJV)

Colossians 1:19–20
For it pleased the Father that in Him all the fullness should dwell, and by Him to reconcile all things to Himself, by Him, whether things on earth or things in heaven, having made peace through the blood of His cross. (NKJV)

Colossians 3:5–10
Put to death, therefore, whatever belongs to your earthly nature: sexual immorality, impurity, lust, evil desires and greed which is idolatry. Because of these, the wrath of God is coming. You used to walk in these ways, in the life you once lived. But now you must rid yourselves of all such things as these: anger, rage, malice, slander, and filthy language from your lips. Do not lie to each other, since you have taken off your old self with its practices and have put on the new self, which is being renewed in knowledge in the image of its Creator. (NIV)

Colossians 3:12–15
Therefore, as God's chosen people, holy and dearly loved, clothe yourselves with compassion, kindness, humility, gentleness and patience. Bear with each other and forgive whatever grievances you may have against one another. Forgive as the Lord forgave you. And over all these virtues put on love, which binds them all together in

perfect unity. Let the peace of Christ rule in your hearts, since as members of one body you were called to peace. And be thankful. (NIV)

Colossians 4:5–6
Be wise in the way you act toward outsiders; make the most of every opportunity. Let your conversation be always full of grace, seasoned with salt, so that you may know how to answer everyone. (NIV)

1 Thessalonians 4:14–18
But I do not want you to be ignorant, brethren, concerning those who have fallen asleep, lest you sorrow as others who have no hope. For if we believe that Jesus died and rose again even so God will bring with Him those who sleep in Jesus. For this we say to you by the word of the Lord that we who are alive and remain until the coming of the Lord will by no means precede those who are asleep. For the Lord Himself will descend from heaven with a shout, with the voice of an archangel, and with the trumpet of God. And the dead in Christ will rise first. Then we who are alive and remain shall be caught up together with them in the clouds to meet the Lord in the air. And thus we shall always be with the Lord. Therefore comfort one another with these words. (NKJV)

1 Thessalonians 5:17
Pray continually; give thanks in all circumstances, for this is God's will for you in Christ Jesus. (NIV)

1 Thessalonians 5:21
Test all things; Hold fast what is good. (NKJV)

2 Thessalonians 2:6
And now you know what is holding him back, so that he may be revealed at the proper time. (NIV)

1 Timothy 2:14
And Adam was not deceived, but the woman being deceived, fell into transgression. (NKJV)

1 Timothy 6:13–16
"…I charge you to keep this command without spot or blame until the appearing of our Lord Jesus Christ, which God will bring about in His own time – God, the blessed and only Ruler, the King of kings and Lord of lords, who alone is immortal and who lives in unapproachable light…" (NIV)

2 Timothy 2:24–26
And the Lord's servant must not be quarrelsome but must be kind to everyone, able to teach, not resentful. Opponents must be gently instructed, in the hope that God will grant them repentance leading them to a knowledge of the truth, and that they will come to their senses and escape from the trap of the devil, who has taken them captive to do his will. (NIV)

2 Timothy 3:16
All scripture is God-breathed and is useful for teaching, rebuking, correcting and training in righteousness, so that the servant of God may be thoroughly equipped for every good work. (NIV)

2 Timothy 4:3–4
For the time will come when they will not endure sound doctrine, but according to their own desires, because they have itching ears, they will heap up for themselves teachers; and they will turn their ears away from the truth, and be turned aside to fables. (NKJV)

Titus 3:4–8
But when the kindness and love of God our Savior appeared, He saved us, not because of righteous things we had done, but because of His mercy. He saved us through the washing of rebirth and poured

out on us generously through Jesus Christ our Savior, so that, having been justified by His grace, we might become heirs having the hope of eternal life. This is a trustworthy saying. And I want you to stress these things, so that those who have trusted in God may be careful to devote themselves to doing what is good. These things are excellent and profitable for everyone. (NIV)

Hebrews 1:14
Are not all angels ministering spirits sent to serve those who will inherit salvation? (NIV)

Hebrews 2:9–18
But we see Jesus, who was made a little lower than the angels, now crowned with glory and honor because He suffered death, so that by the grace of God He might taste death for everyone. In bringing many sons to glory, it was fitting that God, for whom and through whom everything exists, should make the author of their salvation perfect through suffering. Both the one who makes men holy and those who are made holy are of the same family. So Jesus is not ashamed to call them brothers. He says, "I will declare your name to my brothers; in the presence of the congregation I will sing your praises." And again, "I will put my trust in Him." And again He says, "Here am I, and the children God has given me." Since the children have flesh and blood, He too shared in their humanity so that by His death He might destroy him who holds the power of death – that is, the devil – and free those who all their lives were held in slavery by their fear of death. For surely it is not angels He helps, but Abraham's descendants. For this reason He had to be made like His brothers in every way, in order that He might become a merciful and faithful high priest in service to God, and that He might make atonement for the sins of the people. Because He Himself suffered when He was tempted, He is able to help those who are being tempted. (NIV)

Hebrews 5:7–10

During the days of Jesus' life on earth He offered up prayers and petitions with loud cries and tears to the one who could save Him from death, and He was heard because of his reverent submission. Although He was a son, He learned obedience from what He suffered and, once made perfect, He became the source of eternal salvation for all who obey Him and was designated by God to be high priest in the order of Melchizedek. (NIV)

Hebrews 8:7–13

For if that first covenant had been faultless, then no place would have been sought for a second. Because finding fault with them He says, Behold, the days are coming, says the Lord, when I will make a new covenant with the house of Israel and with the house of Judah - not according to the covenant that I made with their fathers in the day when I took them out of the land of Egypt; because they did not continue in My covenant, and I disregarded them, says the Lord. For this is the covenant that I will make with the house of Israel after those days, says the Lord: I will put My laws in their mind and write them on their hearts; and I will be their God, and they shall be My people. None of them shall teach his neighbor, and none his brother, saying, Know the Lord, for all shall know Me, from the least of them to the greatest of them. For I will be merciful to their unrighteousness, and their sins and their lawless deeds I will remember no more. In that He says, "A new covenant", He has made the first obsolete. Now what is becoming obsolete and growing old is ready to vanish away. (NKJV)

Hebrews 9:15–17

And for this reason He is the Mediator of the New Covenant, by means of death, for the redemption of the transgressions under the first covenant that those who are called may receive the promise of the eternal inheritance. For where there is a testament, there must also of necessity be the death of the testator. For a testament is in force after men are dead, since it has no power at all while the testator lives. (NKJV)

Hebrews 9:27
And as it is appointed for men to die once, but after this the judgment, so Christ was offered once to bear the sins of many. To those who eagerly wait for Him He will appear a second time, apart from sin, for salvation. (NKJV)

Hebrews 12:2–11
Let us fix our eyes on Jesus, the author and perfecter of our faith, ho for the joy set before Him endured the cross, scorning its shame, and sat down at the right hand of the throne of god. Consider Him who endured such opposition from sinful men, so that you will not grow weary and lose heart. In your struggle against sin, you have not yet resisted to the point of shedding your blood. And you have forgotten that word of encouragement that addresses you as sons: "My son, do not make light of the Lord's discipline, and do not lose heart when He rebukes you, because the Lord disciplines those He loves, and He punishes everyone He accepts as a son." Endure hardship as discipline; God is treating you as sons. For what son is not disciplined by his father? If you are not disciplined (and everyone undergoes discipline), then you are illegitimate children and not true sons. Moreover, we have all had human fathers who disciplined us and we respected them for it. How much more should we submit to the Father of our spirits and live! Our fathers disciplined us for a little while as they thought best; but God disciplines us for our good, that we may share in His holiness. No discipline seems pleasant at the time, but painful. Later on, however, it produces a harvest of righteousness and peace for those who have been trained by it. (NIV)

James 1:13–14
Let no one say when he is tempted, "I am tempted by God"; for God cannot be tempted by evil, nor does He Himself tempt anyone. But

each one is tempted when he is drawn away by his own desires and enticed. (NKJV)

James 1:17–18
Every good gift and every perfect gift is from above, and comes down from the Father of lights, with whom there is no variation or shadow of turning. Of His own will He brought us forth by the word of truth, that we might be a kind of firstfruits of His creatures. (NKJV)

James 2:20–22
You foolish person, do you want evidence that faith without deeds is useless? Was not our father Abraham considered righteous for what he did when he offered his son Isaac on the altar? You see that his faith and his actions were working together, and his faith was made complete by what he did. And the scripture was fulfilled that says, "Abraham believed God, and it was credited to him as righteousness, and he was called God's friend. You see that a person is considered righteous by what they do and not by faith alone. (NIV)

James 2:26
For as the body without the spirit is dead, so faith without works is dead also. (NKJV)

James 4:17
Therefore, to him who knows to do good and does not do it,to him it is sin. (NKJV)

1 Peter 1:1–2
...To God's elect, strangers in the world, scattered... who have been chosen according to the foreknowledge of God the Father, through the sanctifying work of the Spirit, for obedience to Jesus Christ and sprinkling by his blood: (NIV)

1 Peter 1:20
He indeed was foreordained before the foundation of the world, but was manifest in these last times for you. (NKJV)

1 Peter 2:8
... "A stone that causes men to stumble and a rock that makes them fall." They stumble because they disobey the message – which is also what they were destined for. (NIV)

1 Peter 3:21–22
And this water symbolizes baptism that now saves you also – not the removal of dirt from the body but the pledge of a clear conscience toward God. It saves you by the resurrection of Jesus Christ, who has gone into heaven and is at God's right hand – with angels, authorities and powers in submission to Him. (NIV)

2 Peter 1:21
for prophecy never came by the will of man, but holy men of God spoke as they were moved by the Holy Spirit. (NKJV)

2 Peter 3:8
But beloved, do not forget this one thing, that with the Lord one day is as a thousand years, and a thousand years as one day. (NKJV)

1 John 1:8–11
If we say that we have no sin, we deceive ourselves, and the truth is not in us. If we confess our sins, He is faithful and just to forgive us our sins and to cleanse us from all unrighteousness. If we say that we have not sinned, we make Him a liar, and His word is not in us. (NKJV)

1 John 2:1–2
My little children, these things I write to you, so that you may not sin. And if anyone sins, we have an Advocate with the Father, Jesus

Christ the righteous. And He Himself is the propitiation for our sins, and not for ours only but also for the whole world. (NKJV)

1 John 3:1–3
How great is the love the Father has lavished on us, that we should be called children of God! And that is what we are! The reason the world does not know us is that it did not know Him. Dear friends, now we are children of God, and what we will be has not yet been made known. But we know that when He appears, we shall be like Him, for we shall see Him as He is. Everyone who has this hope in Him purifies himself, just as He is pure. (NIV)

1 John 3:4
Whosoever committeth sin transgresseth also the law: for sin is the transgression of the law. (KJV)

1 John 3:14–15
We know that we have passed from death to life, because we love the brethren. He who does not love his brother abides in death. Whoever hates his brother is a murderer, and you know that no murderer has eternal life abiding in him. (NKJV)

1 John 4:7–9
Beloved, let us love one another, for love is of God; and everyone who loves is born of God and knows God. He who does not love does not know God, for God is love. In this the love of God was manifested toward us, that God has sent His only begotten Son into the world, that we might live through Him. (NKJV)

1 John 4:11–12
Beloved, if God so loved us, we also ought to love one another. No one has seen God at any time. If we love one another, God abides in us, and His love has been perfected in us. (NKJV)

1 John 4:13
By this we know that we abide in Him, and He in us, because He has given us of His Spirit. (NKJV)

1 John 5:19–20
We know that we are children of God, and that the whole world is under the control of the evil one. We know also that the Son of God has come and has given us understanding, so that we may know Him who is true. (NIV)

2 John 1:5–6
And now I plead with you, lady, not as though I wrote a new commandment to you, but that which we have had from the beginning: that we love one another. This is love, that we walk according to His commandments. This is the commandment, that as you have heard from the beginning, you should walk in it. (NKJV)

Jude 1:6
And the angels who did not keep their proper domain, but left their own abode, He has reserved in everlasting chains under darkness for the judgment of the great day; (NKJV)

Revelation 1:5
And from Jesus Christ, the faithful witness, the firstborn from the dead, and the ruler of the kings of the earth. (NKJV)

Revelation 3:21
To him who overcomes I will grant to sit with Me on My throne, as I also overcame and sat down with My Father on His throne. (NKJV)

Revelation 7:2–4
Then I saw another angel ascending from the east, having the seal of the living God. And he cried with a loud voice to the four angels to whom it was granted to harm the earth and the sea, saying, "Do not

harm the earth, the sea, or the trees till we have sealed the servants of our God on their foreheads." And I heard the number of those who were sealed. One hundred and forty-four thousand of all the tribes of the children of Israel were sealed. (NKJV)

Revelation 9:15
And the four angels who had been kept ready for this very hour and day and month and year were released to kill a third of mankind. (NIV)

Revelation 13:8
All inhabitants of the earth will worship the beast – all whose names have not been written in the Lamb's book of life the Lamb who was slain from the creation of the world. (NIV)

Revelation 20:4–6
I saw thrones on which were seated those who had been given authority to judge. And I saw the souls of those who had been beheaded because of their testimony about Jesus and because of the Word of God. They had not worshiped the beast or its image and had not received its mark on their foreheads or their hands. They came to life and reigned with Christ a thousand years. (The rest of the dead did not come to life until the thousand years were ended.) This is the first resurrection. Blessed and holy are those who share in the first resurrection. The second death has no power over them, but they will be priests of God and of Christ and will reign with Him for a thousand years. (NIV)

Revelation 20:12–15
And I saw the dead, small and great, standing before God, and books were opened. And another book was opened, which is the Book of Life. And the dead were judged according to their works, by the things which were written in the books. The sea gave up the dead who were in it, and Death and Hades delivered up the dead

who were in them. And they were judged, each one according to his works. Then Death and Hades were cast into the lake of fire. This is the second death. And anyone not found written in the Book of Life was cast into the lake of fire. (NKJV)

Revelation 21:1–8
Then I saw a "a new heaven and a new earth," for the first heaven and the first earth had passed away, and there was no longer any sea. I saw the Holy City the new Jerusalem, coming down out of heaven from God, prepared as a bride beautifully dressed for her husband. And I heard a loud voice from the throne saying, "Look! God's dwelling place is now among the people, and He will dwell with them. They will be His people, and God himself will be with them and be their God. 'He will wipe every tear from their eyes. There will be no more death' or mourning or crying or pain for the old order of things has passed away." He who was seated on the throne said, "I am making everything new!" Then he said, "Write this down, for these words are trustworthy and true." He said to me: "It is done. I am the Alpha and the Omega, the Beginning and the End. To the thirsty I will give water without cost from the spring of the water of life. Those who are victorious will inherit all this, and I will be their God and they will be my children. But the cowardly, the unbelieving the vile, the murderers, the sexually immoral, those who practice magic arts, the idolaters and all liars – they will be consigned to the fiery lake of burning sulfur. This is the second death." (NIV)

Revelation 21:22
But I saw no temple in it, for the Lord God Almighty and the Lamb are its temple. (NKJV)

ABOUT THE AUTHOR

THE AUTHOR SAYS HE IS NO ONE SPECIAL. HIS FAMILY WAS VERY religious, and his early formative years were filled with religious teaching. Upon graduation from high school, he attended a liberal arts college where he majored in theology and studied all the major religions around the world.

After leaving college he began to realize that much of what he had been taught about the Bible was incorrect and/or non-biblical. He distanced himself from all religions for many years. Eventually he submitted himself to God with a sincere prayer for a relationship with Jesus Christ and God the Father, as well as a request for knowledge, understanding, and faith.

During the following decades he began to conceptualize this book in the hopes it would help others who are struggling to understand their purpose and to follow the straight and narrow path toward eternal life.

He is not currently associated with any church organization due to differences in doctrinal beliefs. He believes his current understanding comes directly from God, through His Word, the Bible, with guidance from the Holy Spirit.[176]

At the time of this printing, he is sixty-seven years old. He feels it is unnecessary to present qualifications for writing this book as the material should stand or fall on its own merits, not because of who wrote it. It is his hope that this work will benefit others by causing them to question their long-standing beliefs and helping develop their faith to higher levels.

---

[176] Acts 2:16–18

Printed in the United States
by Baker & Taylor Publisher Services